Options Trading Simplified For Beginners

Master The Essential Options Skills For
Generational Wealth Even With A Small Account

SimplifiedFor Publications

Before You Go On... make sure to get your Free Gifts!

- Free Ultimate ETF Watch List!

- Free Cost Basis Calculator!

- And More as We Create More Content!
  Just scan or click the QR code below!

http://freegift.simplifiedfor.com

Also, follow our Facebook Page so you can drop us a message or hear about any more Free giveaways!
Scan or click the QR code below to follow!

https://www.facebook.com/WoodleyFuntanilla

Can't wait to hear from you!

Woodley Funtanilla
-SimplifiedFor Publications-

Contents

Introduction

Aww, the hair-raising world of stocks and Options. Like so many people in the investing world, you too may consider these scary, uncharted waters. So much so that people before you have opted to get out of the boat instead of determining the severity of the storm. But it doesn't have to be that way... what if there was no storm at all - but rather a simple adjustment of the sails to be made?

It's no secret that investing in the stock market carries with it some risk. However, it also can bear long-term and even a HUGE upside, which produces rewards to span generations. I will even go so far as to say, that by adding Options to the mix - your potential for growth and wealth expands.

Sounds too good to be true right?

The secret 'sauce' as we'll call it, is simply going into the Options world equipped with a little bit of knowledge on how the relationship between stocks and Options works. This ideal marriage will show you that using Options along with stocks carries much less risk than stocks alone.

That little fact is why I crafted this book.

I've been investing and trading stocks and Options for many years and I've seen first-hand how leveraging this pair is highly beneficial. I've been through ups and downs with the market. I've also worked through many books, online courses, and live training exercises. With this extensive experience, I'm going to show you that Options are not that complicated.

Through the longevity of my own experiences, I've put a lot of effort into turning complicated Option theories into simple and digestible actions. My goal for you is that by the end of this book, you will see that Options are truly less risky than straight stocks, and are far easier to comprehend. If you can calculate plain elementary math - or use the calculator on your phone, then you can succeed with Options.

Ready? Great, now buckle up!

Chapter One

The Markets

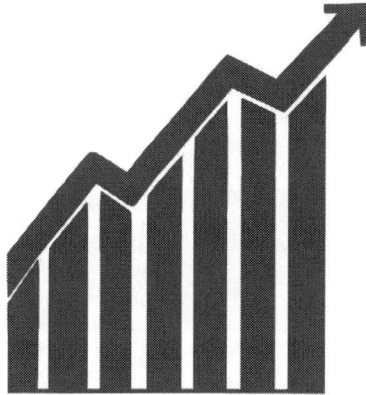

N ow before we take that deep (and maybe scary) dive into the world of Options, I believe with anything else - we should start with the basics. Having a basic understanding of the markets will only help you in the long run.

So what are Options? In a nutshell, Options are contracts that are linked to another asset. These assets can be stocks, indexes, ETFs, currencies, futures, commodities, and basket Options. Understanding these types of assets is essential in understanding Options and how they work. If you are already familiar with these, you can skip ahead to chapter 2... but I also highly suggest reading through them so you have them fresh in your mind during the duration of this book.

What Are Stocks?

Stocks are shares of ownership of a corporation or company. Meaning, the corporation is giving up some ownership of the company to raise capital that will help facilitate future expansion, research and development, and other business expenses. In exchange for this capital, investors may get dividends, voting rights, AND the ability to sell their shares for future profits. These shares typically fall into one of three classes: common (sometimes called ordinary), preferred, or executive. Let's review those.

Common or Ordinary Shares
Just as the name implies, common shares are... well, the most common. These are the types of shares that the general public invests in. They typically have voting rights where one share equals one vote. Common shareholders may also collect dividends and enjoy capital growth.

Preferred Shares
Preferred shareholders may also collect fixed dividend amounts, BUT they give up voting rights. But don't worry - in return for giving up voting rights, preferred shareholders receive these fixed dividends before common shareholders receive theirs. In the case of bankruptcy or liquidation, preferred shareholders are paid before common shareholders. It's a very give-and-take setup.

Executive Shares
Also as the name implies, Executive shares are generally offered to the top decision makers of the company. They carry higher voting weight than common shares, but the ability to sell these shares is quite difficult. In short, it would require board approval to prevent a hostile takeover.

Basically, they just want to ensure the holders of these shares have long term interest in the welfare of the company... which is fair.

Classes of Stock
Classes of stock come in three levels, A, B, and C.

Typical Class Structures
Class A – Common Shares
Class B – Preferred Shares
Class C – Executive Shares

The exact structure of these classes can be customized as the company sees fit. For example, a company may set their Class A Stock to have one vote per share, and their Class C Stock to have 12 votes per share. Dividends will be given to Class B shareholders first, and Class A shareholders will receive any remaining dividends.

What are Indexes?

An index is a statistic that measures the performance of a specific market or sector. It is calculated by taking the weighted average of the prices of all the stocks in that market or sector.

The most well-known market index is the Dow Jones Industrial Average. This index measures the performance of 30 large, publicly traded companies in the United States. Commonly referred to as "The Dow", it's one of the oldest and most widely used market indices in the world. So definitely an index to take note of.

Another popular market index is the S&P 500. This index measures the performance of 500 large, publicly traded companies in the United States. The S&P 500 is often used as a benchmark for investment managers to track their performance against.

There are many other market indexes that measure different markets and sectors around the world. Indexes are commonly used to give an indication of how well a sector or even how the entire market is doing.

What are ETFs?

Exchange Traded Funds, or ETFs - function like mutual funds. They allow investors to pool their money to invest in a variety of stocks. This simplifies automatic diversification and lowers risk. These funds are maintained by money managers in exchange for a small fee based on an expense ratio. The main difference between ETFs and mutual funds is ETFs can be actively traded, just like regular stocks. Whereas mutual funds are not easily traded.

The goal of each ETF is stated in their prospectus. Most ETFs are passively managed. This means that the fund manager tries to closely mimic an index or sector. For example, the ETF SPY closely mimics the stock allocation of the S&P 500. On the other hand, actively managed ETFs give more freedom to the fund managers. Managers tend to move in and out of trades and may move away from basic investment fundamentals like diversification. Actively managed ETFs may have higher returns but come with more risk and higher expenses.

It's important to understand or realize that stocks and ETFs are actual assets. You can own them, trade them, and collect dividends from them. Whereas Indexes are statistical representations of a market or sector. They are essentially benchmarks. You cannot own a benchmark...you cannot own an index. Because of this fact, Options funds are cash-settled at expiration. Instead of settling with shares of stock, index Options convert to the cash value of the Option at expiration. This last sentence will make more sense as you read through this book.

Examples of Index Funds include:

- **S&P 500 INDEX (^SPX)**

- **Dow Jones Industrial Average (^DJI)**

- **NASDAQ Composite (^IXIC)**

- **Russell 2000 (^RUT)**

What Is the Stock Market?

Let's dive into the crazy world of the stock market. Everyone talks about it... but what exactly is it...The stock market is a literal marketplace where buyers and sellers meet to exchange securities like stocks, Options, and ETFs. The entire stock market is made up of various exchanges that facilitate financial transactions for traders. Some of the major stock exchanges include: The New York Stock Exchange, Nasdaq, Shanghai Stock Exchange, The Tokyo Stock Exchange, and The London Stock Exchange. Let's break down how they differentiate from one another.

1. New York Stock Exchange (NYSE)
It is currently the largest stock exchange in the world, consisting of over 2,000 listed companies and having a market capital of more than 22 trillion (USD) as of October 2022. Some of the blue-chip companies listed under it are Coca-Cola, McDonald's, and the Walt Disney Company. Yes, all the big boys.

2. Nasdaq
NASDAQ is an acronym for National Association of Securities Dealers Automated Quotations. It too is an American stock exchange that is based in New York City. At present, it is the second highest on the list of stock exchanges based on the market capitalization of shares traded.

Nasdaq leans technology-heavy, listing some of the largest tech giants such as Apple, Google, Tesla, Amazon, and Microsoft.

3. Shanghai Stock Exchange (SSE)

This Shanghai-based stock exchange is one of the two stock exchanges that operate in China. It is currently the third largest stock exchange in the world, having a market capital of more than 6.8 trillion (USD) as of April 2022.

4. Euronext N.V.

It is a Pan-European stock exchange that offers a variety of trading and post-trade services like custody, settlement, and clearing. Its traded assets include equities, bonds, commodities, derivatives, indices, and foreign exchange. EURONEXT is actually an acronym for European New Exchange Technology.

5. Japan Exchange Group (JPX)

It is a Japanese financial institution that operates the Osaka Exchange, Japan Securities Clearing Corporation, Tokyo Stock Exchange, and Japan Exchange Regulation. Some of the companies listed under it are Toyota, Mitsubishi, Sony, Suzuki, and Honda.

Of course, these are just a handful of the exchanges in the world... there are many other players in the game as well.

The Broker

Retail investors, which just means nonprofessional investors, typically don't trade directly through the exchanges. They go through a brokerage firm. A brokerage firm, or simply put, a broker, is a financial institution that facilitates the buying and selling of stocks and other securities. Brokerage firms are divided into two categories: full-service brokers and discount brokers.

Full-service brokers offer various services, including market research, investment guides, and account management. Discount brokers provide only basic services, such as executing trades on behalf of their clients.

Most brokerage firms require their clients to open an account before they can start trading. Accounts can be opened online or in person at a brick-and-mortar location. When opening an account, clients usually need to deposit a minimum amount of money, which will be used to buy shares of stock.

United States Securities and Exchange Commission
The stock market is regulated by the United States Securities and Exchange Commission (SEC). Its mission is to protect all investors, facilitate the formation of capital, and keep markets orderly, efficient, and of course... fair. Those who buy and sell stocks expect to make a profit through the movements in the stock prices. By maintaining orderliness, the SEC encourages trust in these investment systems.

Three Types of Markets

The buying and selling of stocks happen in three different market types: primary, secondary, and over-the-counter. Let's break each of those down.

The Primary Market
The primary market is where stocks and other securities are first offered to the public, typically done through an Initial Public Offering (IPO). The primary market is important for two main reasons. First, it allows companies to raise capital by selling equity in their business. This is essential for businesses that need money to grow or expand their operations. Second, it provides investors with an opportunity to buy shares in a company before it becomes widely known or successful. This can allow investors to get in on the ground floor of a company and potentially make a lot of money

if the company becomes successful. However, companies typically do not sell to individual investors in the primary market. Instead, they sell to large investors such as hedge funds, mutual funds, and pension boards that manage large amounts of money. After all the shares have been issued, then the primary market closes. Those shares are then offered in the secondary market.

The Secondary Market

The secondary market is a stock market where investors trade securities that have already been issued. When investors talk about the 'stock market,' they usually refer to this secondary market. This market allows many types of investments, such as bonds, real estate, and private equity. The New York Stock Exchange (NYSE), National Stock Exchange (NSE), the London Stock Exchange (LSE), and the NASDAQ are a few secondary market examples. Other smaller exchanges are referred to as over-the-counter markets.

Over-the-Counter (OTC) Markets

Major stock exchanges have requirements that must be strictly met by companies in order for them to qualify for listing. Companies that are not willing or able to meet such standards can go with an OTC sale of stocks. Instead of being listed publicly on a major stock exchange, OTC information is listed on a company website or through brokerages that specialize in trading OTC stocks. There are several reasons why a company might choose to trade OTC instead of on a formal exchange. One reason is that the company may be too small to meet the listing requirements of a formal exchange. Another reason is that the company may be involved in certain types of business activities that would make it ineligible for listing on a formal exchange.

OTC trading can be riskier than trading on a formal exchange since there is less information available about OTC stocks. However, many investors find the extra risk to be worth it since OTC stocks can offer the potential for exponentially higher returns.

Other Types of Markets

Forex

Forex, also known as Foreign Exchange or FX trading, is the act of simultaneously buying one currency while selling another. The goal of Forex trading is to exchange one currency for another in order to make a profit.

For example, if a trader believes that the US Dollar is bullish against the Japanese Yen, they will buy USD/JPY. If their forecast comes true and the USD rises, they will make a profit. On the other hand, if their forecast is incorrect and the US dollar weakens against the Yen, they will lose money.

Futures & Commodities

The futures market is a type of financial market that allows traders to buy and sell commodities or other securities at a predetermined price, the futures price. The commodities market, on the other hand, uses the current price to sell these goods. This is known as the spot price. The most common types of commodities traded in these markets are agricultural products, such as wheat, corn, soybeans, metals, oil, and livestock. Traders use this market to hedge against risk or speculate on price movements in these products. Futures and commodity markets are quite similar. The difference is Futures deal with prices in the future while commodity prices deal with current prices.

Basket Options Market

Basket Options are a type of financial derivative that allows the holder to gain exposure to a basket of underlying assets. The basket can be composed of anything, but typically consists of stocks, commodities, or currencies.

Basket Options are popular because they offer a way to diversify one's portfolio without having to purchase each asset individually. This can be especially helpful in hedging against market risk. For example, if an investor is worried about a potential decline in the stock market, they could purchase a basket Option that includes stocks and other assets that tend to do well in bear markets.

Another advantage of basket Options is that they often have lower transaction costs than buying each asset separately. This is because when you purchase a basket Option you only have to pay one commission, rather than multiple commissions for each individual asset.

Forex, Futures, Commodities, and Basket Options markets are considered exotic Options. For the duration of this book, I will refer to Options trades with traditional Options. These involve stocks, ETFs, and Indexes. Now that you have the basic terms under your belt... let's talk about Options.

Chapter Two

What are Options?

It's time to dive in. As a beginner, I understand that Options concepts may seem quite new and intimidating. That is why I wrote this book, you are not alone - but Options don't have to be intimidating. To give you a little history, you may be surprised to hear that forms of Options trading go way back to the 1600s involving Dutch tulip farmers. I know, wild! I believe it's important to share this with you because even back in those early days and even into the early 1900s, Options trading was very risky because there was no governing body to regulate the sales. Moreover, traders would have to find their own trading partners and haggle prices until a settlement could be reached. It truly was the wild wild west... and for Options trading the era of 'no laws' lasted a long time. But we've grown since that time in the world of trading and while yes, Options are risky, they are no longer the outlaws that they once were.

So what are these financial instruments that traders painfully haggled over? These instruments are insurance contracts that protect against financial loss when the value of a certain commodity falls in price.

Options Are Insurance Contracts

Going back in time, Dutch tulip farmers relied on having a robust season that would provide enough income to sustain them throughout the year. For many of these farmers, if a natural disaster were to sweep across the countryside, their means of survival would have disappeared. Because of this, those farmers could buy an insurance contract on their crops. If disaster did hit, the farmer could be rest assured that they would get some money back for their damaged tulips. Those contracts were the birth of Stock Options.

The buyer of the Option (insurance contract) had the right to the terms of the contract, while the seller had the obligation to the terms of the contract. Because these are contracts, the term buyer is referred to as the holder of the Option. Conversely, the seller is referred to as the writer of the Option. These rights typically involve buying or selling commodities, like shares of stock. Since there are only two "actions" involved with Options (buying and selling), there are only two types of Options: Call and Put Options.

Options contracts that state the right to buy a stock are called Call Options.

Options contracts that state the right to sell a stock are called Put Options.

Call Options

Call Prices Go Up When Stock Price Rises

Now that we know the two types of Options, let's dive deeper into the mechanics of each one. A Call Option represents the right, but not the obligation, to *buy* 100 shares of a certain stock within a certain amount of time. Think of it like a discount coupon. Let's say a rock band is coming to your hometown in six months. The box office price for each ticket is $50. A promoter is selling a coupon for $5 that states that you can buy a ticket for $46 for a $4 savings. You as a smart consumer think that the price of the tickets will actually go up as the date gets nearer and the group gets more popular. You buy one coupon for $5. Six months pass and it is now the day of the concert. You see that the price of tickets has gone up to $75 a seat. Your coupon is now worth much more than the $5 you paid. The value of your coupon is worth the difference between the current price of the ticket and the price printed on the coupon.

When broken down, the math is simple:

$$\$75 - \$46 = \$29$$

You as the smart consumer decide not to go to the concert, but rather to turn around and sell back the coupon for $29. Remember, you paid $5 for the coupon, but because you held the coupon it is worth much more now.

The profit margin on this transaction is:

$$(\$29\text{-}5) / \$5 = 4.8$$

or

Or a whopping
480%

You made a 480% return in six months. Not bad at all. Options are starting to sound a little better now right?

Let's continue this analogy, what happens if the price doesn't change? You as the holder of the coupon still have the right to buy the ticket for $46. You purchased the "option" to either buy the ticket or skip the concert. The "option" is yours. If you still wanted to go to the concert, turn in the coupon and pay $46 for the ticket. The total cost of the ticket is now $51. It may appear you lost $1 in the deal. But what if you changed your mind and decided you didn't want to go to the concert? Life happens and you had to commit to something else. In that case, simply throw away the coupon and move on. You lost $5. But if you bought that ticket 6 months ago, you would be out $50. Personally, I'd rather lose $5 vs $50.

Now picture this...Imagine if the rock band lost their lead guitarist and the ticket price dropped down to $30. You now have the choice. Redeem the coupon to buy the ticket for $46. That doesn't make sense. Go to the concert paying $30 at the box office (a total of $35 with the cost of the original coupon). Or not go to the concert at all and lose the $5. By purchasing the coupon instead of buying a $50 ticket 6 months ago, you'd lose only $5 if you decided to not go to the concert. But if you did decide to go, you actually saved $15 because the price of the box office ticket dropped so much.

The future price of concert tickets does move. The price could drop. But it could also jump many times over. You've seen this happen before as excitement swells around concerts, Broadway plays, or sporting events. With this setup, buying Call Options gives the investor the opportunity to have unlimited profits while keeping risk low. I'm going to say that again... buying Call Options gives the investor the opportunity to have UNLIMITED profits while keeping RISK low.

Now the opposite of Call Options is... Put Options.

Put Options

Put Prices Go Up When Stock Price Falls

A Put Option represents the right, but not the obligation, to *sell* 100 shares of a certain stock, within a certain amount of time. Simply put, Put Options are literally stock insurance contracts between two parties. Think of a car insurance policy. The car owner buys an insurance contract from an insurance agent for six months. The contract states that if the car is damaged causing the car's value to drop to a certain point, the insurance company must buy the car for X amount. The premium that is paid depends on how much the buyer wants to insure. A policy that covers $90,000 will be much more expensive than a policy that covers $50,000. The closer the coverage aligns with the car's actual value, the higher the premium becomes and the lower the risk for the car owner. But, if nothing happens to the car after six months, then the car owner loses the premium they've paid, and the insurance company keeps all the premium as profits.

Within an Option contract, an agreed-upon price is stated, stipulating the price that the holder can buy or sell the asset. This agreed-upon price is referred to as the strike price. In the Call Option example with the concert ticket, $46 is the strike price. In the Put Option example with the car insurance, the amounts of $90,000 and $50,000 are the strike prices. These strikes represent the amount of coverage that the insurance will be responsible for.

Also just like regular insurance coverage, the buyer gets to select the term length. With Options, this is the expiration date. Because the buyer gets to select the term length it is SO important for them to choose it wisely as it can play into your profit... or loss. The longer the term, the more chances the trader gets to be directionally right. But these increased chances will come at a higher cost, in the form of higher premiums. So yes, it is a game of risk as with any trading, but you can be strategic about it.

Here's the kicker though. *You don't have to own the car to buy the car insurance.* You can literally just buy the insurance.

Here's an example. Imagine you're walking down the street and notice a house sitting precariously on a steep slope. Your engineering brain tells you that there is no way that house is still standing in a few months. You go out and buy an insurance contract for that house. A house that you have no rights over! Sure enough, the house topples over and now you can collect the insurance money! Crazy!

Options are Wasting Assets

You'll hear a lot about assets in the trading world, so it's vital you know what an asset is. Fundamentally, an asset is anything that has value that can be bought, sold, or used to generate income. For example, a house is an asset because it can be used for shelter, rented out for profit, or sold for money. A piece of art is an asset because it can be licensed out as reproductions or sold for money. Options are assets like houses and art, but with an expiration date on them. This expiration makes them a wasting asset.

Think of a bushel of fruit. You can buy and sell the fruit. However, if you wait too long, the fruit will rot and eventually not be worth anything anymore. Because Options are assets, you can buy, sell, and trade them like any other asset. You do not have to hold that Option until it 'rots' or it expires. In fact, most Options traders sell back their Options well before expiration.

Options are Derivatives

So just how are Options priced? The price of Options is derived from or follows the price and movement of assets like stocks, ETFs, commodities, indexes, futures, and currencies.

Imagine a person walking a dog. The person is walking in a line. The dog isn't following exactly step by step. The dog can go side to side, lag a little bit, and so on. Overall, the dog stays with the owner. If the owner moves by a certain amount, the dog also moves by a certain amount.

The same holds true for Options. As the price of a stock moves, then its Option will also move. If the price of a stock goes up by $5, then the price of the Option will move by a percentage of that $5. This is where the relationship between the dog and owner comes into play - since an Option is attached to an asset, it cannot "live" on its own. It needs an "owner" just like the dog does.

Underlying Asset of an Option

The underlying is what the derivative is based on. In the example of the dog and the owner, the dog is the Option and the owner is the underlying. Say you buy one Call Option in Apple. Apple is then the underlying asset. This means that the value of the Option, until its expiration, is derived from the price and movement of Apple stock. The value of this underlying asset may change prior to the contract expiration and affect the value of the Option. As a trader, you will be able to know if the Option is worth executing or not based on the value of the underlying asset. Executing the terms of an Option is called *exercising* the Option. They must have known about my dog and owner analogy to call it this. Now that we have this baseline understanding, let's put these concepts together in theoretical contracts so we can come full circle.

Theoretical Call Option Contract

I, *John* (Buyer), holder of this Call Option Contract, reserve the right to buy 100 shares of *Microsoft* (Underlying) for $ *245* (Price/Strike) per share until *Dec 16, 2022* (Expiration). In exchange I will pay $ *10.04* (Premium) per share.

I, *Brandy* (Seller), writer of this Call Option Contract am obligated to sell 100 shares of *Microsoft* (Underlying) for $ *245* (Price/Strike) per share until *Dec 16, 2022* (Expiration), if the holder chooses to execute the terms of this contract. In exchange I will receive $ *10.04* (Premium) per share.

The above Call Option contract means that John now controls 100 shares of Microsoft stock until the end of trading on December 16, 2022. John paid $1,004 for this right. $10.04 is shown. Since one Options contract represents 100 shares, then the premium is worth $1004. John has the Option to buy 100 shares for $245 per share, regardless of what the current market price is. If he exercises this Option, he'll give up the $1004 already paid, and will own 100 shares of Microsoft for $245 per share or $24,500.

Brandy, on the other hand, collected $1004 from John. If John decides to not exercise the contract, then Brandy can keep the $1004. If John exercises the contract, then Brandy will keep the $1004 but must sell 100 shares of Microsoft for $245 per share, regardless of what the current market price is. That is where profit or loss can come into play... regardless of what the market is at the time of expiration. Brandy may be giving up future profits by giving John these rights.

However, both John and Brandy do have the opportunity to buy or sell the contract to another party before expiration, taking any profits or losses at that point.

Now in this analogy, we mentioned names, but it's important to know that the Option writer and holder are not tied to each other. The actual interaction is random. Investors don't know who they are buying from or selling to.

Since we looked at a Call Option contract it's only equitable that we look at a theoretical Put Options contract as well.

Theoretical Put Options Contract

I, _William_ (Buyer), holder of this Put Options Contract reserve the right to sell 100 shares of _Nike_ (Underlying) for $ _92_ (Price/Strike) per share until _Nov 18, 2022_ (Expiration). In exchange I will pay $ _2.44_ (Premium) per share.

I, _Laura_ (Seller), writer of this Put Options Contract am obligated to buy 100 shares of Nike (_Underlying_) for $ _92_ (Price/Strike) until _Nov 18, 2022_ (Expiration), if the holder chooses to execute the terms of this contract. In exchange I will receive $ _2.44_ (Premium) per share.

The above Put Option contract means that William now controls -100 (that's right, negative 100...or short 100) shares of Nike stock until the end of trading on November 18, 2022. William paid $244 for this right. $2.44 is shown. Since one Options contract represents 100 shares, then the premium is worth $244. William has the option to sell 100 shares for $92 per share, regardless of what the current market price is. If he exercises this option, he'll give up the $244 already paid, and will own -100 shares of Nike for $92 per share or $9,200.

Laura, on the other hand, collected $244 from William. If William decides to not exercise the contract, then Laura can keep the $244. If William exercises the contract, then Laura will keep the $244, but must buy 100 shares of Nike for $92 per share, regardless of what the current market price is.

As in the Call Option, both William and Laura have the opportunity to buy or sell the contract to another party before expiration, absorbing any profits or losses.

Reasons for Buying Options

Now that you see Options broken down and have a better understanding of them, it's good to know why traders choose to buy Options. For Options buyers, there are two main reasons why they use Options vs straight stock: *leveraged speculation* and *hedging*.

Leveraged Speculation

Of course, profits are what everyone is after. So, how do Options traders make their profits? Speculators make predictions on which way a stock might move in the future. Typically, if an investor thinks a stock will rise, then they buy a Call Option. If they think the stock will fall, they buy a Put Option.

Let's say Apple is currently trading at $170 per share. A speculator predicts Apple stock will go up in the next few weeks. This speculator may purchase 100 shares for about $17,000. If the stock rises by $5, then the investment goes up by $500 or a 2.9% gain. Not bad. Now instead, the investor buys a Call Option. A one-month Call Option near the current share price is $450. *Note: these actual figures come from Apple's Option table at the time of this writing. I'll go over "reading" an Options table later in this book.* This means that with $450, the investor controls 100 shares of AAPL for 30 days. If the stock rises by $5, then the Option price will go up to about $765. That's a 70% jump from $450. This leverage gives investors great gains if they are correct... *if* they are correct on their prediction. You will notice that the rise in the Option was $315 vs $500 when trading straight stock. Because Options are derived from the underlying, the price changes won't be equivalent. It will generally be lower.

Now on the flip side, if an investor believes a stock will fall in price, they will buy Puts instead of buying Calls.

Hedging

Hedging is another word for "betting the other way." Back to talking about insurance policies... An insurance policy acts as a hedge. You can treat Options as if they are insurance policies to protect investments in case a downturn occurs. Purchasing Put Options will allow you to reduce your risk of crashes without affecting the benefits of owning stock, i.e. dividends or future growth.

Let's say you own 100 shares of Merck. You have a bad feeling about the economy, so you want to insure your investment from a large drop in stock price. You can buy a 30-day Put Option like an "insurance policy" that protects you if Merck drops below a certain price. The price or premium of this insurance is based on how close the coverage is to the current stock price and the number of days of coverage. Just like before with our insurance analogy, the higher the coverage, the more expensive it is. In addition, the more days of coverage the more the cost goes up.

If you are a short seller, you can buy Call Options to limit your losses in case the price of the underlying goes against you during a short squeeze.

What is a short seller? Short selling is when investors sell stocks they don't own. They borrow the shares from other investors in the hopes that the price of the stocks drops. If/when the price drops, then they buy it back at a lower market price, profiting from the difference.

American Style Options vs European Style Options

When you first start trading Options, you'll see two styles available to you. European style Options and American style Options. Here's a quick rundown of their differences.

European Style Options:
1. Exercise Limitation: European style Options can only be exercised on the expiration date.
2. Flexibility: These Options offer less flexibility to the holder since they cannot be exercised before expiration.
3. Pricing Consideration: Pricing of European Options is usually determined using mathematical models, such as the Black-Scholes model, which assumes no dividends are paid during the Option's life.

American Style Options:
1. Exercise Flexibility: American style Options can be exercised at any time before the expiration date.

2. Price Volatility: Due to their flexibility, American style Options generally demand a higher premium than European style Options.

3. Dividend Impact: The timing and amount of dividends may impact the decision to exercise an American Option early.

The *main* difference that you need to focus on between European and American style Options is that European Options can only be exercised at expiration, while American Options provide greater flexibility by allowing exercise at any time before expiration. For the remainder of this book, Options will be explained with the American style in mind.

We've gotten through the basics of Options... congratulations you made it! We'll be getting into the weeds now and honestly, the fun part.

But wait, let's test your newfound knowledge...

Get out your thinking cap; it's test time.

Options can be thought of as?
1. Insurance contracts
2. Concert tickets
3. Bank notes
4. Farmer's crops

You can hold an Option forever
1. True
2. False

Another word for executing the terms of an Option is?

1. Sell

2. Buy

3. Exercise

4. Obligate

In American style, when can the holder exercise the Option?

1. Two trading days after expiration

2. Only if the seller agrees

3. Any time before the end of trading on expiration day

4. Only on expiration day

One Call Option controls how many shares of stock?

1. 125

2. 150

3. 1

4. 100

One Put Option controls how many shares of stock?

1. 125

2. -100

3. -1

4. 100

Which statement is true?

1. A holder sells an Option to a writer.

2. A writer sells an Option to a holder.

Practice Test Answers

Options can be thought of as?

*1. Insurance contracts

2. Concert tickets

3. Bank notes

4. Farmer's crops

You can hold an Option forever

1. True

*2. False

Another word for executing the terms of an Option is?

1. Sell

2. Buy

*3. Exercise

4. Obligate

In American style, when can the holder exercise the Option?

1. Two trading days after expiration

2. Only if the seller agrees

*3. Any time before the end of trading on expiration day

4. Only on expiration day

One Call Option controls how many shares of stock?

1. 125

2. 150

3. 1

*4. 100

One Put Option controls how many shares of stock?

1. 125

*2. -100

3. -1

4. 100

Which statement is true?

1. A holder sells an Option to a writer.

*2. A writer sells an Option to a holder.

Chapter Three

Moneyness

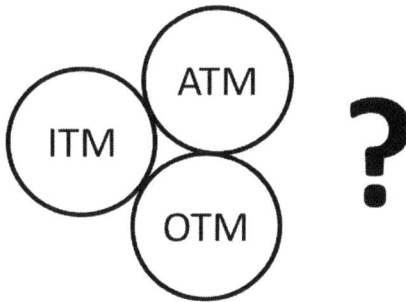

I t's a fun term to say... but what exactly is Moneyness? Moneyness refers to the relationship between the current price of an underlying asset and the strike price. It can also be thought of as the likelihood of an Option having any value at expiration vs. expiring worthless. That is simply put, but let's break it down beyond laymen's terms. It all starts with the Strike Price.

Importance of the Strike Price

The strike price is the agreed-upon price that the writer is willing to buy or sell the underlying for.

In a Call Option, the *lower* the strike price, the more expensive the Option becomes. In the coupon analogy, let's say you have a group of 3 coupons that you can purchase which will give you a discount for a concert. The original ticket price costs $50. One coupon will give you the right to buy the ticket for $30. Another will give you the right to buy the ticket for $40. And the last coupon will give you the right to buy the ticket for $45. The price for the $30 coupon will be more expensive than the $45 dollar coupon. This is because the buyer is getting a bigger discount.

In a Put Option, the *higher* the strike price, the more expensive the Option becomes. In the car insurance analogy, you have a group of 3 insurance levels that you can purchase which states, if your car is damaged and is worth less than the insurance level, then the insurance company will buy your car at the insured rate. Your car is currently worth $50,000. One level will give you the right to sell the car for $30,000. Another will give you the right to sell the car for $40,000. And the last level will give you the right to sell the car for $45,000. The price for the $45,000 insurance level will be more expensive than the $30,000 insurance level. This is because the car owner will receive more money for the car if it is damaged.

Let me be clear though, Strike prices are set. Investors cannot create their own "coupons". But rather, investors are given a list of available strikes per underlying.

In terms of Moneyness, the important components of the Options contract are the underlying's current price and the strike.

Going back to laymen's terms:

- **Underlying's Current Price**: Current price of the asset linked to the Option.

- **Strike**: The price at which the holder can buy or sell the underlying asset.

The relationship between the underlying price and strike price determines its Moneyness. The term Moneyness is a way of describing how close the strike price is to the current underlying price. Think of an auto mechanic feeling the hood of a car to determine if the car is overheating. The scale, using a heat index instead of numbers would be:

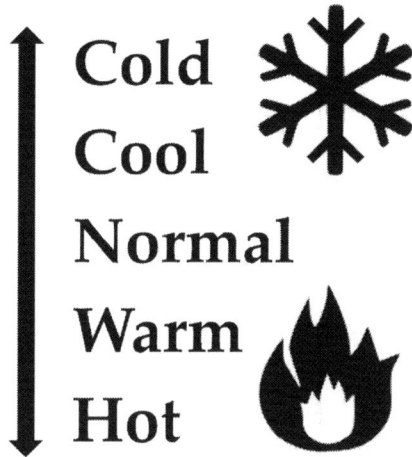

Cold
Cool
Normal
Warm
Hot

Fig 3a. Temperature Index

If the car is cool, then it's probably running fine. But if it is hot, then the likelihood of something being mechanically wrong is extremely high. Without stating exact temperatures, a mechanic can easily describe the state of the car. Moneyness does the same thing in Options lingo with the scale being:

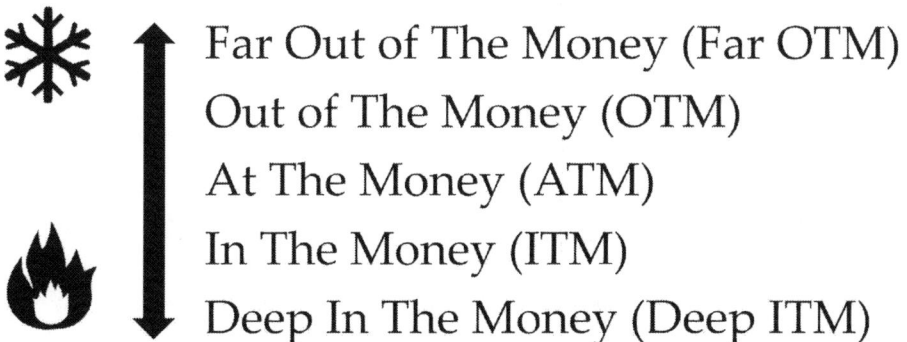

Far Out of The Money (Far OTM)
Out of The Money (OTM)
At The Money (ATM)
In The Money (ITM)
Deep In The Money (Deep ITM)

Fig 3b. Temperature of Options

Take time to memorize OTM, ATM, and ITM. You'll be using them a lot.

With the example of the car's temperature, the goal is to determine if it will overheat. With Options, the goal is to determine if an Options contract is likely to be exercised or if it will expire worthless. You can say Moneyness is a thermometer for the Option. The *hotter* the Option gets, the more likely it will be exercised. Hotter Options are also more expensive. The *colder* the Option is, the more likely it will expire worthless. Colder Options are also cheaper.

Moneyness (Temperature) of Options

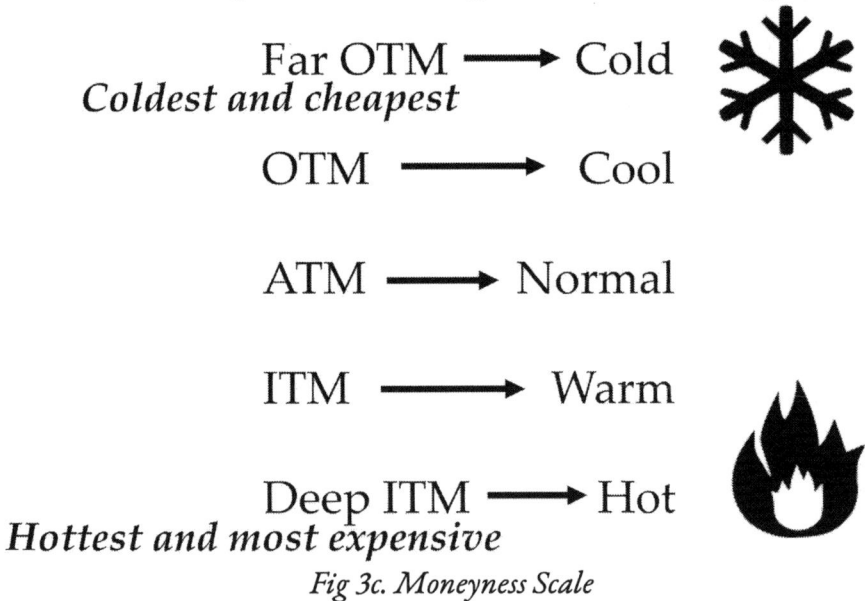

Far OTM ⟶ Cold
Coldest and cheapest

OTM ⟶ Cool

ATM ⟶ Normal

ITM ⟶ Warm

Deep ITM ⟶ Hot
Hottest and most expensive

Fig 3c. Moneyness Scale

Moneyness in Call Options

An ITM Call Option means that the strike price is below the asset price by at least $.01. Any strikes above the current asset price is OTM.

Consider this example. Apple is sitting at $145 per share. The Option strike at 145 will be ATM. Strikes below 145 will be ITM. Strikes above 145 will be OTM. As the price of Apple moves, so does the relationship between the strikes and its Moneyness.

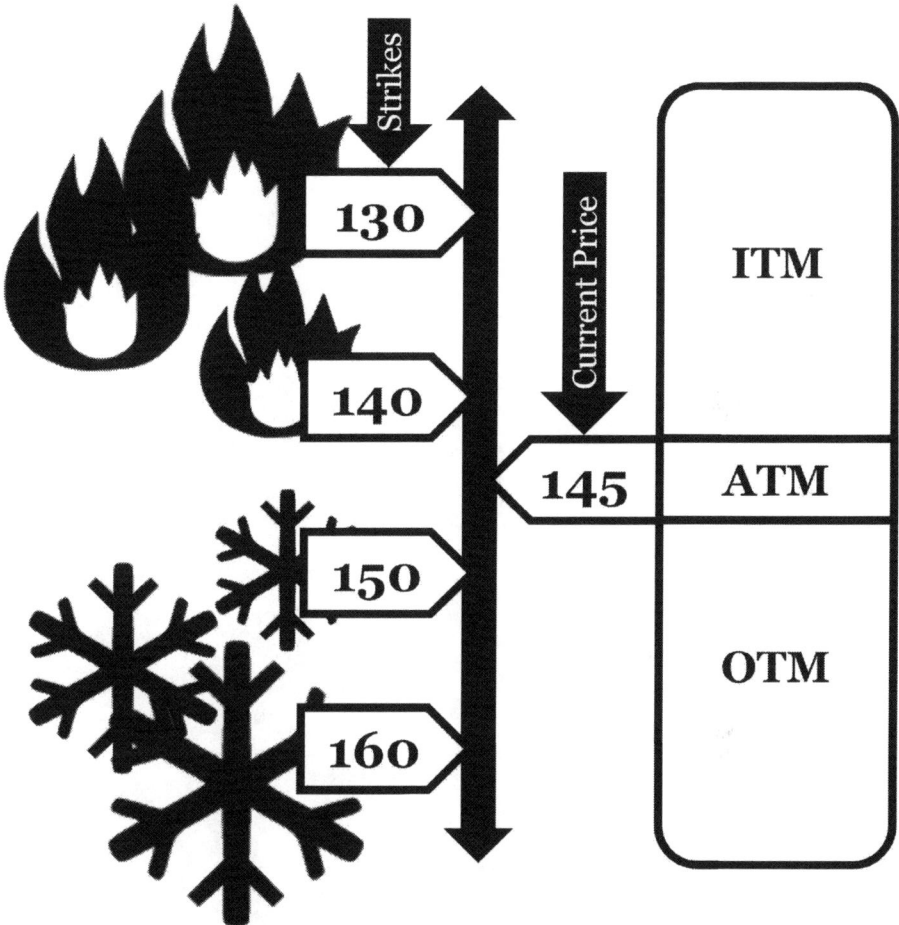

Fig 3d. Moneyness in Call Options

As the graphic above shows, the 140 strike is ITM. What happens if Apple drops to 138? That means the 140 strike will become OTM. The 150 and 160 strikes will go further than OTM.

If Apple rises to 157, then the 150 strike becomes ITM. The 130 and 140 strikes will go deeper into ITM.

Moneyness in Put Options

The Moneyness relationship is the opposite for Puts vs. Calls.

An ITM Put Option means that the strike price is above the asset price by at least $.01. Any strikes below the current asset price are OTM.

Going back to Apple, it is sitting at $145 per share. The Option strike at 145 will still be ATM. Now for Puts, strikes above 145 will be ITM. Strikes below 145 will be OTM.

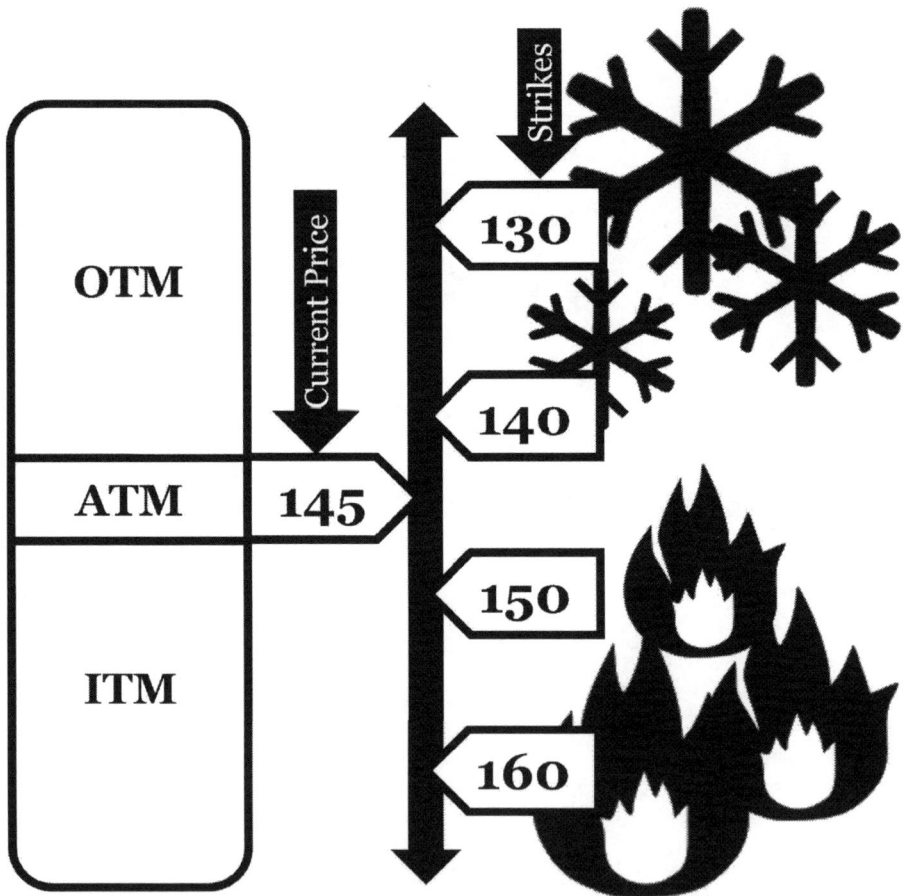

Fig 3e. Moneyness in Put Options

What happens if Apple drops to 138? That means the 140 strike will become ITM. The 150 and 160 strikes will go further ITM. If Apple rises to 157, then the 150 strike becomes OTM. The 130 and 140 strikes will go further into OTM.

The reason why it's so vital to fully understand Moneyness and finding the Moneyness of strikes, is that it is key to assessing risk before submitting a trade. The relationship between the temperature of an Option is directly linked to the amount of risk a trader is taking on. The hotter the Option, the higher the risk...but it comes with more potential reward. So in our temperature scale, risk also slides as the temperature slides up and down.

Expiration Cycles

Remember going over expirations in Options? Well, expirations fall into several categories of expiration cycles that are pertinent to know, and are simple to remember based on their category title. They are:

•Standard Monthlies

•Weeklies

•Monday & Wednesday Weeklies

•Quarterlies

Standard Monthlies

These are the baseline Option expirations. If Options are available for an underlying, they will start with Standard Monthly Options. Standard Monthly Options expirations happen every third Friday of the month. If that Friday falls on a trading holiday, then the previous Thursday becomes the expiration day.

Weeklies

Weeklies expiration cycles are the same as monthlies. The only difference is that they expire every Friday. As underlyings become popular, weeklies are added to give investors more choices for trading. On many trading platforms, you can distinguish an expiration as a weekly Option with the letter "W" next to the expiration date.

Monday & Wednesday Weeklies

Within the weekly expiration cycle family, there are Monday weeklies and Wednesday weeklies. These are added for large indexes and ETFs like SPY, QQQ, IWM, and SPX. The treatment of these contracts is the same as monthlies and weeklies. Monday & Wednesday weeklies expire, as you may have guessed... on Mondays and Wednesdays.

Quarterlies

Again, the same treatment as the other above expiration cycles. The difference being the expiration day falls on the last trading day of the month. These expirations are also reserved for large indexes and ETFs. As with the others, if the last day of the month is a Holiday, then the expiration date is the day prior. The birth of quarterly expirations started as a hedge for large financial institutions that operate on a quarterly accounting basis. Quarterly expirations can be pointed out on a platform with the letter "Q" next to the expiration date.

Why Options Expiration Day is Important

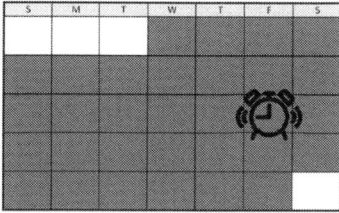

Options expiration day gives many investors feelings of anxiety. At the end of trading on expiration day, the Moneyness determines if the Option will be exercised or not. All ITM Options are automatically exercised after expiration day, whether the investor is the holder or the writer. The panic comes in when investors fail to close a position and are now stuck with an obligation that they can't carry.

To give you an example, let's say you're holding a Call Option in Apple with strike 100. Apple closes at a share price of $100.01 on expiration day. If nothing is done, you will be stuck with 100 shares of Apple costing $100 per share or $10,000. You may or may not be able to afford this amount. You must then scramble to either sell those shares first thing the next trading day, hoping that the price doesn't fall. Or you must deposit enough funds to carry the position.

On the opposite end, holders of OTM Options will feel the pinch of the wasting asset. On expiration day, all values of OTM Options will evaporate. They will expire worthless. OTM Options holders will have to decide if they want to let these contracts expire worthless, or try and sell them back just to make a few dollars in return. Many times the transaction fees will eat this profit, so most traders tend to let them expire on expiration day.

If investors understand the implications of holding positions through expiration day, there should be no stress or worry. To reduce this worry, most Options traders close positions before expiration day, accepting any profits or losses. As a beginner, closing trades early is the way to go. If you've been watching your underlying for many months, years, or decades, you start to get a *feeling* of the potential price movements of the stock. These observations will add to your skills to determine if your positions are in danger or not.

I hope you are starting to see why Options seem scary and complicated from the outside, but really are not... it just takes a full understanding of them and how they 'play with others' to then use this knowledge to your advantage. It's like the old saying goes, 'you don't know what you don't know.' But on the flip side, knowledge is power... so turning what you don't know into full understanding sets you up for playing the game strategically. Which is really how the Options world works.

Let's practice what you've just learned!

The current price of XOM is 110. The 113 Call is:
1. ITM
2. OTM
3. ATM
4. Deep ITM

The current price of FRT is 104. The 50 Put is:
1. ITM
2. ATM
3. Far OTM
4. OTM

The current price of GD is 219. The 190 Call is:
1. ITM
2. Deep ITM

3. ATM

4. OTM

The current price of EMR is 83.25. The 83 Put is:

1. ITM

2. ATM

3. OTM

4. Deep ITM

The current price of JNJ is 151. The 175 Call is:

1. ITM

2. Far OTM

3. Deep ITM

4. ATM

Expiration day just ended and HRL closed at 38.18. The 38 Call Option:

1. Will get exercised

2. Will expire worthless

Expiration day just ended and AAPL closed at 157.83. The 160 Call Option:

1. Will get exercised

2. Will expire worthless

Expiration day just ended and BA closed at 196.12. The 195 Put Option:

1. Will get exercised

2. Will expire worthless

Expiration day just ended and IWM closed at 171.56. The 172 Put Option:

1. Will get exercised

2. Will expire worthless

Practice Answers

The current price of XOM is 110. The 113 Call is:

1. ITM

*2. OTM

3. ATM

4. Deep ITM

The current price of FRT is 104. The 50 Put is:

1. ITM

2. ATM

*3. Far OTM

4. OTM

The current price of GD is 219. The 190 Call is:

1. ITM

*2. Deep ITM

3. ATM

4. OTM

The current price of EMR is 83.25. The 83 Put is:

1. ITM

*2. ATM

*3. OTM

4. Deep ITM

In this case, the answer could be either 2 or 3. Most Traders will call that ATM.

The current price of JNJ is 151. The 175 Call is:

1. ITM

*2. Far OTM

3. Deep ITM

4. ATM

Expiration day just ended and HRL closed at 38.18. The 38 Call Option:

*1. Will get exercised

2. Will expire worthless

Expiration day just ended and AAPL closed at 157.83. The 160 Call Option:

1. Will get exercised

*2. Will expire worthless

Expiration day just ended and BA closed at 196.12. The 195 Put Option:

1. Will get exercised

*2. Will expire worthless

Expiration day just ended and IWM closed at 171.56. The 172 Put Option:

*1. Will get exercised

2. Will expire worthless

Chapter Four

Options Premium and The Greeks

L ittle refresher, Options are insurance contracts. And just like home-owners insurance or car insurance, we the owners need to pay the piper to protect our assets. The cost of this insurance is called the premium. Likewise, the cost or value of an Option is also referred to as its premium. When a holder buys an Option, they're paying the premium to the writer. The premium is comprised of two parts, the Intrinsic and the Extrinsic value.

Intrinsic Value

Intrinsic Value is the difference between the strike price and the underlying price. Only ITM Options have any intrinsic value. Once the strike is OTM, then it has zero intrinsic value. For example, let's say you have a Call Option in Apple with strike 160. The current price of Apple is $150. Holding this Option gives you the right to buy 100 shares of Apple for $160 per share. Would you execute it? Absolutely not! Why pay $160 per share when the current market price is $150? Meaning this Option has no intrinsic value. If you held the Call Option at strike 140, then you would be getting a discount if you executed the Option. $150-$140=$10. This Option has $10 of intrinsic value. The deeper ITM an Option is, the higher the intrinsic value. The rest of the Options premium comes from extrinsic value.

Extrinsic Value

Extrinsic Value is the added value given to Options. It's calculated by subtracting the intrinsic value from the current Options price. If an Option is OTM, then all of the premium is extrinsic value. This added value is a type of 'sweetener' in the Options premium. The pricing of Options needs this sweetener to give some benefit to the Options writers. If no benefits exist for the Options writer, no one would take the other end of the deal. It's equivalent to the world of sports gambling. A bookie will add odds to a bet so that both sides have perceptually even chances of winning. Otherwise, who would take the bet?

To take it a step further, imagine a basketball team, The Juggernauts, comprises all-stars. They've been crushing teams by 40 points every night. The next game is against the worst team in the league, The Slugs, with zero wins to their name. The betting line could say:

The Juggernauts -50 over The Slugs.

This means that The Juggernauts must win by more than 50 for this bet to win. If The Juggernauts beat The Slugs by 48, this bet loses. Now, if the line said:

The Juggernauts -1 over The Slugs

No one would take the other side of the bet. Everyone would bet on The Juggernauts.

Extrinsic value works the same way. Value must be added to the Options premium to make it worth it for the writer. Remember, the writer of the Option is taking on the obligation of the contract. This obligation has a price. That is its extrinsic value. The different factors that go into the extrinsic value Options premium have a term... it is known as The Greeks. No, it doesn't come from nationality, but rather think back to the good old College days and the sororities and fraternities with Greek letters.

The Greeks

These Options factors are a set of five main influencers, or measures which are named after Greek letters. They boil down to how sensitive an Option is as we spoke about before. Such factors include time, changes in volatility, and movements in the price of the underlying security.

Delta

Diving right into it... it's only fair we start with Delta. As Delta is the most important Greek. It measures the change in an Option's price given a one-unit up move in the underlying asset. It tells you how much an Option's price will move if the underlying stock goes up by $1. Delta can be positive or negative. It varies depending on the type of Option, Call or Put. If you held a Call Option with a Delta of .40, then if the stock moves up by $1, the Option will go up by $.40. The opposite holds for Put Options. A Put Option with Delta -.40 will move -$.40 for every $1 movement up a stock makes.

Remember, Options represent 100 shares. If a stock goes up by $1, then the investment goes up by $100. If an Option goes up by $.40, then the investment goes up by $40. One does not equal one in Options, one equals one hundred.

ATM Options have a Delta around 0.50 for calls and -0.50 for puts. As you move deeper ITM money, Delta will increase for Call Options and decrease for Put Options. Eventually, deep ITM Calls and Puts will mimic actual stock and short stock movement. Some investors refer to holding deep ITM Options as holding synthetic stocks. They are not buying actual shares, but their Options are so deep that the Option price movements almost fluctuate dollar per dollar with the share price. Deep ITM Options can have Delta .80 or more for Call Options or -.80 or less for Put Options.

Delta is also popularly used as a measuring stick to measure the probability of the Option expiring ITM. An Option with Delta .80 has an 80% chance of expiring ITM. An Option with Delta .10 has a 10% chance of expiring ITM. Options traders use Delta as a quick shorthand to determine if a trade is worth it or not. The caveat is that Delta is not always right. As we know from previous chapters, things change during the lifecycle of an Option. Consider this analogy - during a newscast, the meteorologist will give a weather forecast with a percentage of the likelihood of rain. The forecast may say there's a 20% chance of rain - therefore, there is an 80% chance of sunshine. You like those chances and leave the umbrella at home. Just your luck, the meteorologist was wrong, and a storm cloud rolls in, drenching you on your way into the office.

This scenario is parallel to how Delta operates. As you make decisions on whether to buy or sell Options, using the Delta is a great way of helping you finalize your choices. But don't use it as your only input to determine your trade decisions. Just as you wouldn't live your life based solely on what the meteorologist said... You may get wet in the end.

Vega

Vega, V, is volatility. I like to think of Vega as how bi-polar a stock is. If an underlying's price is constantly shooting up and quickly crashing down, then it's a volatile stock. If the stock price moves nice and smooth, then not so volatile. Of course, this is a simplified definition.

In technical talk, the method in which Vega is calculated involves two inputs, Historical Volatility (HV) and Implied Volatility (IV). Start with Historical Volatility (HV). To get an indication of how a stock will move in the future, we must look at the stock movement in the past year. Volatility is basically a measurement of movement. This movement is the propensity for a stock's price to swing above or below its mean throughout a specific time period, i.e. one year.

Implied Volatility (IV) is a product of HV along with strike price, the volatility of the stock, the time to expiration, and the interest rate. These factors are used in various pricing mathematical models to output IV. One of the most popular pricing models is the Black-Sholes Pricing Model.

Black-Sholes

I know you are curious, so here's a brief explanation of Black-Sholes. In the early 1970s, Fischer Black and Myron Scholes developed a model for pricing Options. The model, now called the Black-Scholes model, is used by traders to determine the fair price of an Option. The Black-Scholes model is based on the assumption that the price of a stock follows a random walk. This means that the stock price can be thought of as a random process that evolves over time. The model also assumes that there is no risk-free rate of return and that all investors are risk-averse.

Using the Black-Scholes model with the various inputs, IV is calculated. Once this implied volatility is found, this measurement is then used to find Vega. Vega expresses the correlation between a 1% change in Implied Volatility to the Option price. If an Option has a Vega of 0.20, it means that its price should increase by $0.20 when the underlying asset's volatility increases by 1%. With Delta, an underlying price increase will cause the Call Delta to go up and the put Delta to go down. With Vega, a volatility increase in the underlying will cause both the Call and the Put to increase in Vega. Vega causes both the Call and to Put to increase because it measures the magnitude of IV, not the direction.

The actual mathematical model is complex. Luckily for you, Vega and IV are already presented to you when you look at an Options Chain (Options Chains are coming up next chapter).

In practice, investors use IV and Vega as indicators of how risky an Option is. The higher the IV, the more the risk. But along with more risk, there is more reward if the Option moves in your favor. You can also think of Vega as the measurement of "Frenzy" or "Fear" in the stock. If a certain stock activity jumps because suddenly everyone started selling, Vega increases. If everyone started buying like crazy, Vega, again, would increase.

Theta

θ Theta is the rate of decline in the value of a Call or Put Option with the passing of time. It's easier to think of Theta as the "time decay" of an Option. When all other factors are held constant, the Option's Theta will show you the daily decay of the premium. If an Option has a Theta of -3, then the Option will lose $3 per day. Theta is always negative for both Calls and Puts. The closer the Option is to expiration - the value of

Theta sharply declines. Refer to the image below to see how the rate of Theta decay increases as expiration nears.

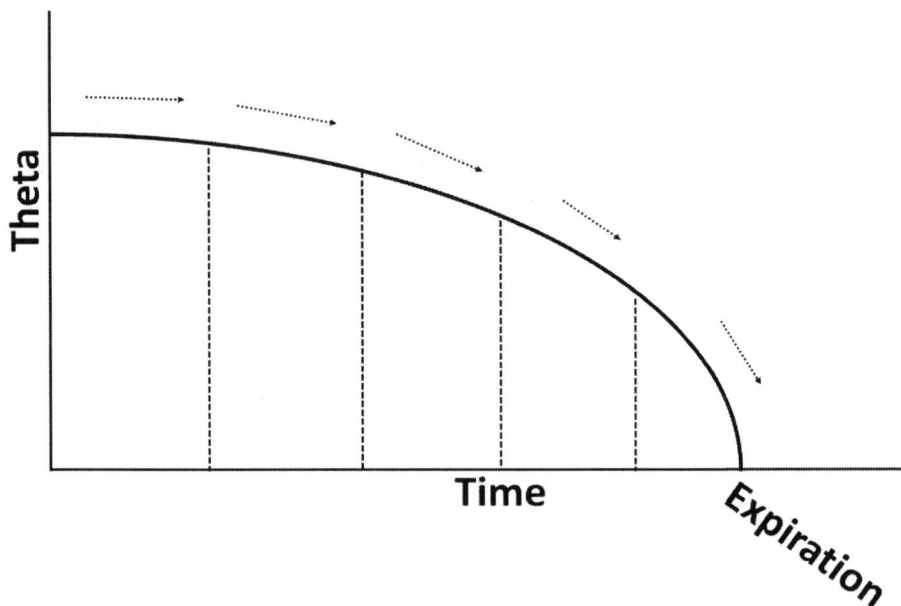

Fig 4a. Movement of Theta

Gamma

γ Gamma refers to the rate of change in an Option's Delta, in relation to changes in the underlying asset. As you'll remember, Delta is a measure of an Option's price sensitivity to changes in the underlying asset. Gamma is often referred to as a "second-order" Greek because it measures the rate of change in Delta or its acceleration.

Gamma is positive for both Call and Put Options when the underlying asset price is changing. Also, as the underlying price gets closer to ATM, then Gamma rises. The further away the underlying is from ATM, then Gamma falls. The important thing to know about gamma is that it truly kicks in toward the end of the Option's life. As the effect of theta quickly diminishes at the end, the effect of gamma quickly increases at the end.

Think of those coin-wishing wells. We drop a coin and it spins down the slope. The closer it gets to the bottom, the faster it spins. That's how gamma works... you have to wait till it's deathbed to see the profits or losses come to fruition.

Rho

In finance, the rho (/roʊ/) is a measure of the sensitivity of the price of an Option to a change in interest rates. Rho measures the amount by which an Option's price changes when interest rates move higher or lower. Generally speaking, Call Options will see their prices increase when interest rates rise, while Put Options will become more expensive when rates go down.

The Greeks are important because they allow investors and traders to understand how an Options position might react to changes in things like volatility, time to expiration, and interest rates. This understanding is critical when it comes to making sound trading decisions and managing risk. Reference these two images to visually see the relationship between Options Price and Intrinsic Value, Extrinsic Value, and the Greeks.

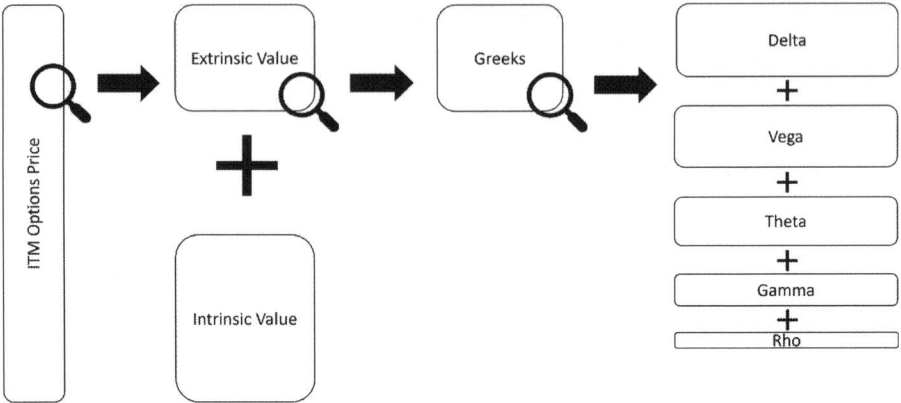

Fig 4b. In The Money Options Pricing

Compare ITM Pricing construction above and the below OTM Pricing construction. They are basically the same, except OTM Options have no Intrinsic value.

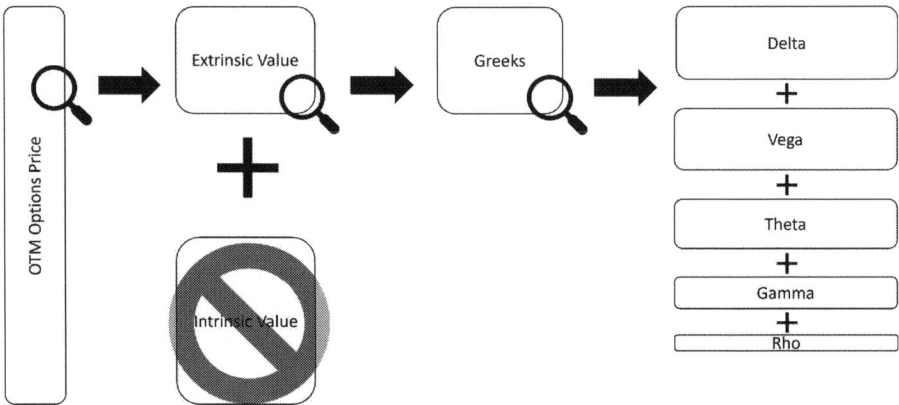

Fig 4c. Out Of The Money Options Pricing

Earnings and Vega

You may already know that publicly traded companies give quarterly or yearly financial updates to investors, media, and analysts. These updates are referred to as earnings reports or paper reports, and earnings calls which is a speech presentation followed by a Q&A. Within these calls and reports, executives tell shareholders how well or poorly the company is doing. The SEC requires companies to file either a form 10-Q (quarterly) or 10-K (yearly) report detailing the financial health and also any future guidance regarding where the company, industry, or economy is heading.

Before the actual report comes out, analysts predict what will be in these reports and create target Earnings Per Share (EPS) goals for the call - commonly referred to as Consensus EPS. EPS is calculated as Net Income minus Preferred Dividends

If the call exceeds the Consensus EPS, then the company Beat the Consensus. This is usually followed by a rise in stock price. If the call is below the Consensus EPS, then the company Missed the Consensus. This is usually followed by a fall in stock price. These events "usually" happen, but with the nature of the markets, the actual stock price may not follow this pattern. As an investor, be prepared to see these deviations occasionally.

As Options buyers and sellers, holding positions with expirations through earnings does pose issues. Earnings reports are supposed to be kept secret until the actual earnings release date. Investors and analysts are left "guessing" what the report will say about the company. This uncertainty brings about a level of fear within the public. Regarding Options, this fear is closely linked to Vega and IV. The more fear there is, IV goes up causing Options prices to go up. Once earnings calls are over, fear dissipates, and IV drops. This is often referred to as IV crush. During this time, you may hold an Option worth $100 before the earnings call. The trading day after the earnings call, that Option may drop by 20, 30, or even 50% just because of this IV crush. Yikes!

Many investors who choose to trade through earnings tend to be Options sellers. When opening a trade as a seller, the goal is to buy the Option back at a lower price. This crush will go in the investor's favor if the stock moves in the right direction or if the stock doesn't move much. Many traders refer to trading around earnings as Earnings Trades. Trades with expirations beyond the earnings date will have Vega inflated. As soon as the Earnings Report comes out, Vega deflates.

Some traders avoid earnings trades by soley trading ETFs. Less to worry about.

Now that we're coming up for air from being thick in the weeds of Options terms and how they play together - be sure to bookmark this chapter for reference down the road. The fun part of trading Options and the process is just around the bend.

Review Questions Time!

All OTM Options have Intrinsic Value.
1. True
2. False

All ITM Options have Intrinsic Value.
1. True
2. False

Options Premium is made up of
1. Intrinsic Value + Extrinsic Value
2. Intrinsic Value + Extrinsic Value + Future Value
3. Extrinsic Value + Strike Price

When the underlying price moves up, Call Delta moves which way?

1. Down

2. Up

3. Stays the same

When the underlying price moves up, Put Delta moves which way?

1. Down

2. Up

3. Stays the same

Volatility increase will cause Call Vega to increase, and Put Vega to decrease.

1. True

2. False

Theta can be considered the "time decay" of an Option.

1. True

2. False

Which Greek takes interest rates into consideration?

1. Gamma

2. Rho

Delta

Alpha

If you want to enter an Earnings Trade, you should select expirations that expire when?

1. Before the earnings date.

2. After the earnings date.

Practice Answers

All OTM Options have Intrinsic Value.
1. True
*2. False

All ITM Options have Intrinsic Value.
*1. True
2. False

Options Premium is made up of
*1. Intrinsic Value + Extrinsic Value
2. Intrinsic Value + Extrinsic Value + Future Value
3. Extrinsic Value + Strike Price

When the underlying price moves up, Call Delta moves which way?
1. Down
*2. Up
3. Stays the same

When the underlying price moves up, Put Delta moves which way?
*1. Down
2. Up
3. Stays the same

Volatility increase will cause Call Vega to increase, and Put Vega to decrease.
1. True
*2. False
Volatility causes both Call and Put Vega to go up.

Theta can be considered the "time decay" of an Option.

*1. True

2. False

Which Greek takes interest rates into consideration?

1. Gamma

*2. Rho

3. Delta

4. Alpha

If you want to enter an Earnings Trade, you should select expirations that expire when?

1. Before the earnings date.

*2. After the earnings date.

Chapter Five

Reading the Option Chain

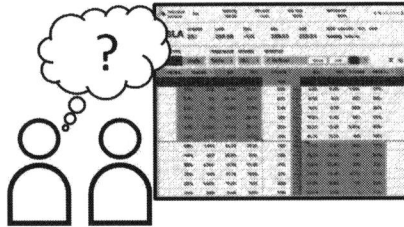

L earning the mechanics of executing an Options trade takes a lot of knowledge, patience, and practice. The great news is you are reading this book, so by the end of reading this you can cross number one off this list.

The other great bit of news is that both patience and practice can be achieved by anyone, you just have to be willing to put in the work and the effort. Think back to when you first sat behind the wheel of a car. You stared at the console, afraid to touch anything. Your instructor walked you through the major parts that you would be working with, the brake pedal, steering wheel, gas pedal, and so on. Learning and identifying the different mechanisms while in the driver's seat is essential for any new driver. Buying and selling Options takes the same amount of patience and practice. The driver's seat for Options is called the Option Chain.

Now, think back to the most recent time you drove a car. You didn't even think about where the turning signal was or where the gas pedal was, you just went through the motions because your body and mind have been trained to do so. How? From years and years of patience, practicing how to drive. Options trading is the same.

Every broker presents the Option chain a little differently. The ability to identify the important sections of the chain will make it easier to properly execute trades and migrate to different brokers if needed. For all my visual learners out there, a typical chain will look like this chain from TD Ameritrade (soon merging with Charles Schwab).

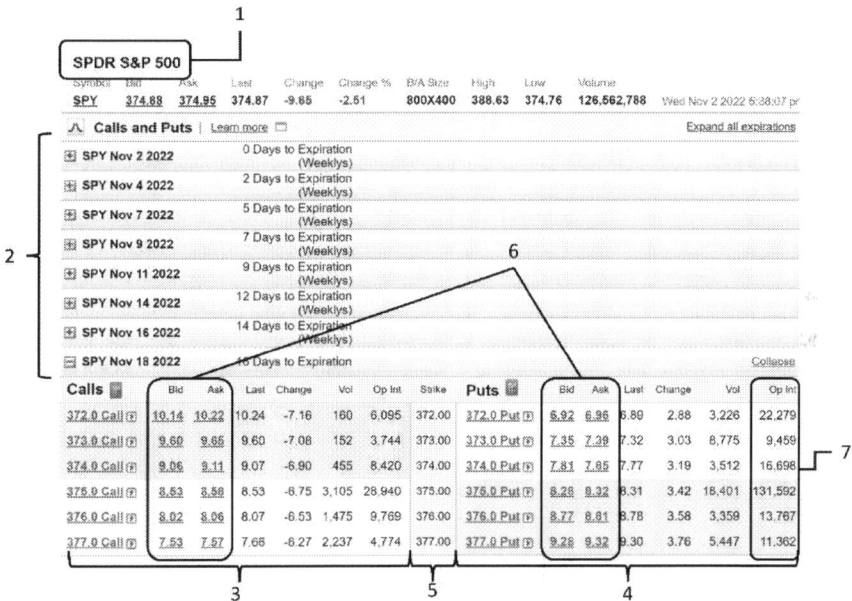

Fig 5a. The Options Chain

Before you get overwhelmed, let's dissect the parts. Remember, you've already learned the theory of these parts, and now you can see them in action.

1. **Underlying**. Underlying selection is the first thing you must de-

cide before making a trade. You will typically see the underlying stated at the upper left of the trade screen. In this example, the underlying is the S&P 500, symbol SPY.

2. **Expirations**. Remember, you need to make note of what expiration dates you choose. Unlike buying and selling straight stock, traders can't hold Options forever. Traders must have a preconceived notion of if and when these stocks will make moves.

3. **Calls**. Calls are shown on the left side of the chain.

4. **Puts**. Puts are shown on the right side of the chain.

5. **Strikes**. Available strikes will be between the Calls and the Puts. Note how the strikes are ordered. Lowest strikes are at the top, higher strikes are at the bottom. This may take a little getting used to because of how we perceive the pricing of stocks. It's one of those things that you'll adjust to with time.
   *Some platforms may allow you to change this sort order

6. **Bid/Ask**. Selecting the bid/ask on the chain will determine if the trader is a buyer or a seller. When traders click on the bid price, they are *selling* the Option. When traders click on the asking price, they are *buying* the Option.

7. **Open Interest**. This shows how many open contracts are available.

Beyond these 7 items, the Option chain can be manipulated to show all types of values, including all of the Greeks. Customize the platform to show any metric to help you make trading decisions.

Now that you can breathe a sigh of relief because it's really not as scary as it looks - it's time to put these individual pieces together to create a story of the trade. We'll start first with selecting the underlying.

Liquidity of Underlyings

What makes a good underlying to trade Options in? Liquidity. Liquidity is another way of showing how popular a certain stock is. Popularity doesn't necessarily mean everyone thinks it's going up or going down. What it means is there are a lot of people interested in holding positions in that underlying.

To determine liquidity with the Option chain, two values should be looked at: Open interest and bid/ask.

Open Interest

Open interest is the number of outstanding contracts for that specific strike. The higher the number, the more liquid. In the example, SPY is the underlying. SPY also happens to be one of the most traded underlyings out there. Millions of transactions per day are made with SPY. This is evident with such high open interest numbers. Pay close attention to the strikes that are close to ATM on both the Call and Put sides. This is where most of the action takes place.

Bid/Ask

The other indicator for liquidity is looking at the bid/ask. To do this you must first analyze the bids for the OTM Options right at the current underlying price. If the bids are near 0, that means there are no buyers. No one is bidding for those contracts. Conversely, look at the ask right next to the bid. If the ask is far from the bid price, then that means there is no agreement between the buyers and the sellers. Ideally, a trade will happen when the seller and the buyer agree on price. This typically happens at the midpoint of the bid and the ask, conveniently called the mid-price. The difference between the bid and the ask is called the bid/ask spread. The larger the spread, the less liquid the underlying.

Think about the stock market in general. It's basically a big auction market, like eBay. Let's say you have an old camera that you would like to get a few bucks for. So you put out a description of the product and your asking price, the price you hope to get for the product.

Gently Used Camera
Asking $55

You, the seller, put out an asking price of $55. You wait a few days, but no one is taking it. You look at other listings with the same camera and find that the ones that are selling are going to a lower bid price of $45. You mark down your camera to the lower bid price, and it finally gets sold. The same transaction happens with stocks and Options.

Asking price of $55
Bidding price of $45
Mid price of $50

This means that if you priced the camera at $50 you have a greater chance of it getting sold than if you listed it at $55. If you listed it at $45, it will pretty much guarantee it will get sold, but you take a $10 hit on the price. So like there is give and pull in the market of selling products, there is in the stock market. It is all based on the 'market value' or what your 'competitors' are listing their items for. If you put yourself in the buyer's shoes, why would you buy a camera for $55 when you see the exact same camera being sold for $45?

Why is liquidity so important?

Favorable Fills

With bid/ask spreads, the wider the bid/ask, the more of a hit traders will take as either a buyer or a seller. The tighter the spread, the less of a hit they will take. These hits can add up in the long run. Tight bid/ask spreads would be about 5-20 cents. Anything beyond that may make the trade not worth it. You could potentially lose $30 or $40 per trade just on wide spreads.

Remember, you must add the opening trade and the closing trade. And with wide spreads, finding a trading partner becomes more difficult. Let's say you had to buy back your Option to avoid assignment. If there is no one willing to sell to you at a reasonable mid-price, then you'd be forced to buy it back at the higher asking price. Getting favorable fills will save you hundreds or even thousands of dollars throughout your trading journey.

Predicting the Future

Using the data in the chain is useful to decide what underlying to trade. It is also useful to give traders a glimpse into how likely an outcome is to occur based on past data. One of the most popular methods is using Delta.

Delta

I know, I know, this is feeling like deja vu. But I want to show you how Delta comes into play again. As a refresher from Chapter 4, Delta can be used to get an approximation if an Option will expire worthless or not. If you convert the Delta into a percentage, then subtract it from 100. A Call Option with a Delta of .10 will have a 90% chance of expiring worthless at expiration. A Put Option of -.30 will have a 70% chance of expiring worthless at expiration. You'll notice that ATM Options have around a .50 Delta value. This makes sense because then there would be a 50/50 chance of those Options expiring worthless. Which is also the same winning chance you get if you were to buy the stock at that price, 50/50.

A common use of Delta is finding the standard deviation of the stock movement.

One Standard Deviation represents a range that includes approximately 68% of all price outcomes. Two Standard Deviations represent approximately 95% of all pricing outcomes.

Some platforms conveniently show 1 STD (Standard Deviation) and 2 STD right in the Option chain. This is usually evident with a line running in between the strikes where the STD lay. But some platforms may not show these standard deviations. To quickly determine where these lines are, use Delta.

On the Call side, a Delta with a number between .10 and .15 will be about 1 STD from the current underlying price. A Delta of about .03 will be approximately 2 STD from the current underlying price.

Whereas on the Put side, a Delta with a number between -.10 and -.15 will be about 1 STD from the current underlying price. A Delta of about -.03 will be approximately 2 STD from the current underlying price.

Keep in mind, these values are specific for that exact point in time with the exact market/business/sector conditions. Any changes happening in the market will affect the Delta, therefore those predictions will not be 100% accurate. Use Delta as a guide, not as a Bible.

Expirations and Strikes

Another way of looking into the future is using the expirations and strikes to predict premium movement. Let's say you had information on BMY to make a move in the next 30 days. The current price for BMY is $80.28. The 80 Call with 30 DTE (days to expiration) costs $1.84. Look at the same strike with 16 DTE. That Option is priced at $1.40. This means that if the price of the stock doesn't move and about 15 days go by, then your Option will lose $.44 in value. To simulate the stock moving up by $1, look at the Option 16 DTE, call strike 79. That has a value of $2.03. This means that if you bought the 80 Call with 30 DTE and BMY moved up $1 within 15 days, then your Option will be worth about $2.03 for a profit of $19 or a 10% increase.

Again, this is shorthand for predicting the future. Using this method will give you an idea of how much your stock must move and in what time frame to make a profit. Also, note that using this technique does not consider things like vega or gamma. Both Greeks will affect premium pricing.

*Some trading platforms offer "future" testing built in. Consult your broker to see if they have this capability. Personally, I like to use this technique that I laid out because it's quick and easy to implement. No need to change screens or input values.

Your Choices as an Options Investor

Options traders' mindsets are multi-dimensional. When breaking all these concepts down, you will notice that there are five things that you can control in Options contracts.

1. Underlying
2. Option Type (Call or Put)
3. Strike
4. Expiration
5. Quantity

Evaluating these five elements before executing a trade is paramount in becoming a successful trader. Without full knowledge of what to select can doom you from the beginning.

Selecting the Underlying

In selecting the underlying, I strongly suggest you work with stocks or ETFs that you will be proud to own for a long period of time. Minimum 5 years. With this mindset, you'll find and invest in companies that align with your personality and future financial goals. Would you own part of a company that you know nothing about or don't agree with their business practices? Are you comfortable with being a shareholder of a company that regularly uses child slave labor to produce its goods? Would you buy shares of a company that continually has bad earnings reports or uses questionable accounting practices to boost the books? If you go the ETF route, select funds that you have some interest in or working knowledge of. Let's say you are a nurse working in a hospital setting. You have a good working knowledge of the medical field and can see what products and services are doing well within that industry. In this case, you may want to use the fund XLV as an underlying because it focuses on the healthcare sector. Getting stuck in losing trades is horrible. Getting stuck in losing trades with companies or ETFs that you were never interested in owning is a nightmare.

Keep the following in mind when selecting underlyings.

1. Good liquidity

2. A company you are familiar with and have extensively researched
   a. Steady cash flow and profits
   b. Moderate levels of debt
   c. Good management teams
   d. Strong moat

3. Sector (ETF) you are familiar with

4. An entire market index like SPY, if you just want to go with the market

Option Type Selection

So with all this information, should you buy or sell a Call or a Put? This question depends on your future outlook on the stock. If you are bullish, either buy a Call or sell a Put. If you are bearish, either sell a Call or buy a Put. The next chapter will focus on analyzing the risk of each type of position. When you understand the risk, the right decision becomes apparent.

Strike Selection

The bottom line for strikes is, to choose strikes that you are comfortable with. This choice can be connected to the Moneyness of the strike. Remember, the more ITM a strike is, the higher the premium. The higher the premium, the higher the risk. The higher the risk, the higher the reward if you are directionally right. The opposite of course is, the higher the risk the higher the loss. Your understanding of how individual stocks or ETFs move throughout various events can greatly aid you in making this decision. You can get this knowledge from observing the market for a period of time, and identifying trends and levels of resistance. Using technical or fundamental analysis can help you make these decisions. Other traders use services that feed them trading ideas. Whatever path you choose, selecting the right strike is a decision you cannot take lightly. Let's say 3M is trading for $126. You sell a 125 Put Option for $4 per share. Are you willing to own 100 shares of 3M for $125 per share or $12,500? If you are not comfortable with this scenario, choose a strike that is further OTM. The premium you collect will be less, but the risk will drop. Take into account the worst-case scenario when selecting strikes. In this example, the worst case is you will own 100 shares of 3M at $125 per share. Are you comfortable with that? Make sure you accept this risk before pushing submit. Careful strike selection is crucial.

Expiration Selection

How confident are you that you will be directionally right before expiration? Remember, as the expiration of Options nears, the premium value from Theta decay eats at the price. If you are also wrong directionally, the Option premium value drops exponentially. The more time you give yourself, the better chances you have of being correct. Keep in mind, the cost of this time is a higher premium.

Also, always consider earnings dates, new product releases, world events, etc. If you know a significant event is coming up, factor that into your expiration selection. If you want to stay away from an event, select a date *before* that event. If you want to take advantage of that event, select a date *after* that event.

Significant events affect Options through Vega. The crazier the event, the more Vega is activated. If you're an Options seller, you want to stay away from these events because your goal is to buy back the Options at a lower price. As an Options buyer, you want more Vega so you can sell back the Options at a higher price. One more note about expirations and Vega. If the upcoming event is planned or "everyone" knows about it, then the Vega is already priced into the Options price. It will be difficult to game the system thinking you're going to outsmart the market with known events.

Here's an example. Say you bought a Call Option in Apple with an expiration beyond the date that the new iPhone will be introduced. You paid $300 for this Option. You're thinking that there's no way this iPhone will bomb. It'll be huge! Fast forward...the iPhone is introduced with a wonderful reception. You expect your Option will be worth much more now. You check your account and it's unchanged. What happened? At the time you purchased the Call, market makers already *baked in* the event into the Options price. Any advantages you thought you had disappears. Just remember, when pricing Options, the market accounts for everything.

Quantity Selection

Many beginner Options traders are drawn to the possibility of exponential growth from small investments. The possibility of turning a $20 Option investment into a $200 dollar investment within a few days is real and achievable. That 1000% increase sounds quite enticing. If it's possible, why not buy 2 Options at that price and double the winnings? What about buying 1,000 Options at that price and turn $20,000 into $200,000? But is that type of growth sustainable in the long run? No. Eventually, simple math kicks in. Remember, the Delta of Far OTM Options (the cheap ones) are quite low. Hence the probability of those contracts moving near ITM is also low. Math will kick in and those probabilities will go against you. Just because an Option is cheap, doesn't mean it's a good investment.

The possibility of exponential growth should never tempt investors to buy more Options that they really can't afford. The more Options you buy, the more risk you're putting on the table.

The same is true for Options sellers. Selling Far OTM positions may sound less risky. But since the premiums are so low, there is the temptation to sell more contracts than you can truly afford if the position went against you.

The point here is, to be mindful of how many contracts you buy and sell. This number could give you nice returns, or easily break your bank.

Dividends

Trading through dividends also causes issues with Options traders. More specifically, this affects traders that buy or sell Calls, but not so much Puts. Dividends are given to shareholders that hold stock positions before a certain date. This date is called the Ex-Dividend date. Any new shareholders on or after that date will not get the dividend. As Call Option holders, the decision must be made: Can I benefit from exercising my Option early, buying 100 shares, and receiving the dividend? The larger the dividend, the more appealing early exercise may be.

The opposite end is the Call Option writer. They carry the risk of the holder exercising early. This is called Dividend Risk. If they sold 1 Call Option and that Option got exercised early, then they must sell 100 shares and miss out on the dividend.

Some brokers automatically exercise Options if it will go in the trader's favor. This auto-exercise setting is usually something that must be manually turned on by the investor. Consult your broker if you're interested in turning this feature ON.

Reading the Option Chain is a good way of determining if your position is worth exercising as a holder, or if your position is in danger of dividend risk. Here's how to do it. Look at your short Call position. Now go across and look at the corresponding Put position. Look to see if the Put is less than the expected dividend. If the Put is less than the expected dividend, then there is a high chance of an early exercise.

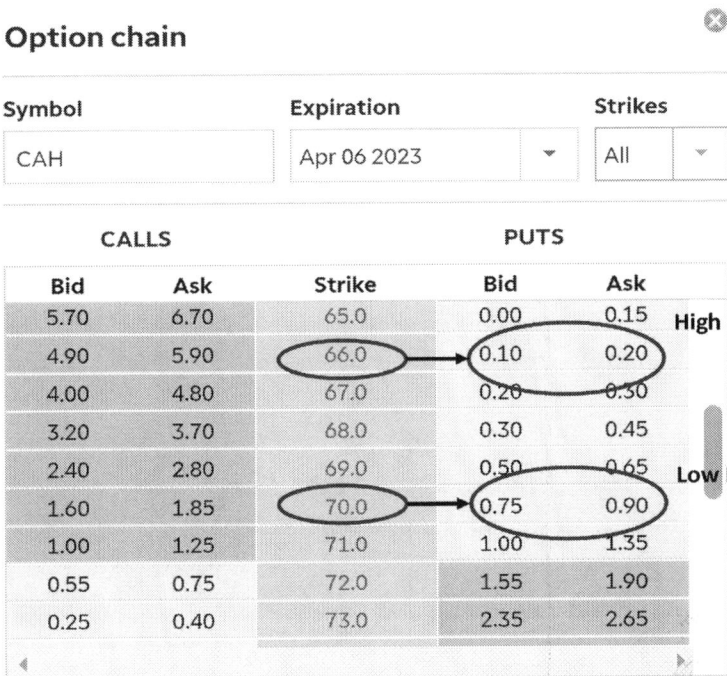

Option chain

Symbol	Expiration	Strikes
CAH	Apr 06 2023	All

CALLS			PUTS	
Bid	**Ask**	**Strike**	**Bid**	**Ask**
5.70	6.70	65.0	0.00	0.15	High Dividend Risk
4.90	5.90	66.0	0.10	0.20
4.00	4.80	67.0	0.20	0.30
3.20	3.70	68.0	0.30	0.45
2.40	2.80	69.0	0.50	0.65	Low Dividend Risk
1.60	1.85	70.0	0.75	0.90
1.00	1.25	71.0	1.00	1.35
0.55	0.75	72.0	1.55	1.90
0.25	0.40	73.0	2.35	2.65

Fig 5b. Dividend Risk

In this example, CAH has an upcoming dividend of .495 per share. The Option at Strike 66 has a high chance of assignment because the corresponding Put is lower than the dividend. The Option at strike 70 has a lower chance of assignment because the corresponding Put is higher than the dividend. Again, this is shorthand. The Option holder can execute their contract at any time before expiration *and for any reason*. Using this technique is pretty safe, but just be mindful that it's not 100% foolproof.

Let's see what you've learned.

Calls are typically on the?
1. Right side of the chain
2. Center of the chain
3. Left side of the chain

Puts are typically on the?
1. Right side of the chain
2. Center of the chain
3. Left side of the chain

Strikes are typically on the?
1. Right side of the chain
2. Center of the chain
3. Left side of the chain

Open Interest and Bid/Ask spread is important because?
1. Shows the volatility of the underlying
2. Shows which way the market is moving
3. Shows how liquid an underlying is
4. Not important at all

A Call Option with Delta .3 has what percent chance of expiring worthless?
1. 30%
2. 80%
3. 70%
4. 0%

A good company to invest in will NOT have?

1. Steady cash flow and profits
2. High levels of debt
3. Good management teams
4. Strong moat

A Call Option with high dividend risk will have a corresponding Put that's?

1. Higher than the dividend
2. Lower than the dividend
3. No correlation
4. Depends on IV

Answers

Calls are typically on the?

1. Right side of the chain

2. Center of the chain

*3. Left side of the chain

Puts are typically on the?

*1. Right side of the chain

2. Center of the chain

3. Left side of the chain

Strikes are typically on the?

1. Right side of the chain

*2. Center of the chain

3. Left side of the chain

Open Interest and Bid/Ask spread is important because?

1. Shows the volatility of the underlying

2. Shows which way the market is moving

*3. Shows how liquid an underlying is

4. Not important at all

A Call Option with Delta .3 has what percent chance of expiring worthless?

1. 30%

2. 80%

*3. 70%

4. 0%

A good company to invest in will NOT have (multiple answers)?

1. Steady cash flow and profits

*2. High levels of debt

3. Good management teams

*4. No moat

A Call Option with high dividend risk will have a corresponding Put that's?

1. Higher than the dividend

*2. Lower than the dividend

3. No correlation

4. Depends on IV

Chapter Six

Analyzing Trade Risk: BE, MP, ML

Improper risk assessment can quickly turn a promising trade into a losing trade. Traders must fully realize what can happen with a trade during the worst-case scenario. With any type of investment, emotional reactions to the market's upswings and downturns will make traders do "stupid" things. Getting into the mindset of learning to be comfortable with downturns and having enough knowledge to mitigate and adjust trades is key.

Think about other aspects of your life... before making a major decision to move to another state, buy a house, or change jobs you would weigh both the pros and cons. You would also look at the long-term effects it would have on your life and if you would be happy with those outcomes whether good or bad. So is true when analyzing risk, you must look beyond the horizon and see if you can handle both the good outcome and the possible bad outcome. Can you live with it - is what you should constantly ask yourself.

To properly assess risk in an Options trade, you must be able to figure out three important calculations. These are Break Even Point (BE), Maximum Profit (MP), and Maximum Loss (ML).

When calculating these values, ensure you understand that these calculations are for Options at expiration. By doing this you know how much you can lose and how much you can gain per trade. Then you can make educated calculations on how much profit to take to close trades before expiration. Fortunately, this skill only involves basic math.

You may have already figured out that there are only four types of Options trades that an investor can make.

1. Buy Call

2. Sell Call

3. Buy Put

4. Sell Put

When buying an Option, the investor is giving cash to the writer of the Option. This is known as a debit. When selling an Option, the investor is receiving cash from the holder. This is known as a credit.

Transactions are also noted as opening or closing trades. An opening trade is the initial trade that is made to start the position. If an investor buys to open (BTO) a position, this is referred to as a long position. The investor is the holder of the Option. If an investor sells to open (STO) a position, this is referred to as a short position. The investor is the writer of the Option. Broken down it would look like this:

Buy = Long = Option Holder = Debit

Sell = Short = Option Writer = Credit

A closing trade is done to close the position. If the initial trade was sell Put, then the closing trade will be buy Put. Acronyms BTC (buy to close) and STC (sell to close) are used by traders for closing trades.

The four types of trades have different calculations for Max Profit, Max Loss, and Break Even.

Long Positions Risk

Long positions are the easiest trades that beginners can conceptualize. They operate the same way you buy and sell material goods – Buy Low & Sell High. You buy a house for $300,000. Sell the house a few years later for $350,000. Profit $50,000. The same holds for Options. Buy a Call for $5.00 in hopes the Option price goes up before expiration. The Option jumps to $6.00...sell. Let's look at the math of the different types of trades.

Long Call Calculation

Max Profit	Unlimited
Max Loss	Premium Paid per share x 100
Break Even	Strike + Premium Paid per share

Example:

Andrew believes EEM stock price will rise. He buys a Call Option in EEM for $.89 at strike 35. The current price of EEM is $34.77

Max Profit	Unlimited
Max Loss	$.89 x 100 = $89
Break Even	35 + .89 = $35.89

Max profit is unlimited because there is theoretically no limit to how high EEM can go before expiration. The most Andrew can lose in the trade is the $89 premium he paid upfront. For Andrew to make at least 1 cent from the trade, the stock price must move up and over $35.89 at expiration.

Long Put Calculation

Max Profit	(Strike - Premium Paid) x 100
Max Loss	Premium Paid x 100
Break Even	Strike - Premium Paid

You'll notice that the profit loss calculations for Put Options are the opposite of Call Options. This is because Put Option values go up as the stock price goes down.

For Example:

Sally believes TSLA stock price will fall. She buys a Put Option in TSLA for $13.55 at strike 225. The current price of TSLA is $224.64

Max Profit	(225 - 13.55) x 100 = $21,145
Max Loss	$13.55 x 100 = $1355
Break Even	225 - 13.55 = $211.45

Max profit is $21,145. This is achieved if TSLA went bankrupt at expiration. The most Sally can lose in the trade is the $1,355 premium she paid upfront. For Sally to make at least 1 cent from the trade, the stock price must move down and below $211.45 at expiration.

Short Positions Risk

Short positions are a bit trickier to conceptualize. They operate the opposite of Buy & Sell. Instead of Buy Low & Sell High, short positions follow Sell High & Buy Low. Let's say a short seller sells a Put for $6.00 in hopes the Option price goes down before expiration. The Option drops to $5.00...buy it back.

Short Call Calculation

Max Profit	(Premium Received) x 100
Max Loss	Unlimited
Break Even	Strike + Premium Received

For Example:

Ronald believes CVX stock price will fall or stay the same. He sells a Call Option in CVX for $4.80 at strike 180. The current price of CVX is $177.09

Max Profit	$4.80 x 100 = $480
Max Loss	Unlimited
Break Even	180 + 4.80 = $184.80

The Max profit is $480. This is achieved if the CVX stock price stays below $180. The most Ronald can lose in the trade is infinite because there is theoretically no limit on how high CVX can go. For Ronald to make at least 1 cent from the trade, the stock price must stay below $184.80 at expiration. As a beginner, do not, I repeat, do not sell Calls in stock you do not own. This is referred to as selling Naked Calls. The max loss is literally unlimited... yes you read that correctly, UNLIMITED LOSS.

Short Put Calculation

Max Profit	(Premium Received) x 100
Max Loss	(Strike - Premium Received) x 100
Break Even	Strike - Premium Received

For Example:

Cindy believes JNJ stock price will rise or stay the same. She sells a Put Option in JNJ for $1.01 at strike 165. The current price of JNJ is $172.21

Max Profit	$1.01 x 100 = $101
Max Loss	(165 - 1.01) x 100 = $16,399
Break Even	165 - 1.01 = $163.99

Max profit is $101. This is achieved if JNJ stock price stays above $165. The most Cindy can lose in the trade is $16,399. This will happen if JNJ went bankrupt. For Cindy to make at least 1 cent from the trade, the stock price must stay above $163.99 at expiration.

Here is where a lot of traders fall into the blinded trap. Unlimited profits attract many beginner traders to hold long Call/Put positions. If a trader is right directionally, yes, buying Calls and Puts will work. But therein lies the caveat...The trader must be right directionally. Just like you look both ways when crossing a one-way street, you must look both ways here. Yes, one way looks and should be fine, but you still check the other direction to be safe.

Limited profits repel many beginner traders from short Call/Put positions. Add the large amount of risk put on the table if the trade goes bad. Because of this, beginners will have a hard time starting with selling Options. But the difference between buying Options and selling Options is the trader does not have to be 100% directionally right. In the next chapter, I will go over trading techniques that limit risk and allows traders to profit, even if the trader is wrong directionally. Yes, that is possible.

Cheat Sheet		
Bullish	Buy Call	Sell Put
Bearish	Sell Call	Buy Put

Fig 6a. Options Cheat Sheet

Options Shorthand

Options traders use a type of shorthand to simplify their transactions log. Keeping a log of your trades is useful and necessary when trading Options. Logging your trades will give you a wide-eyed view of what strategies are working and what strategies need to be reevaluated. If you join any Options groups on Facebook or other social media platforms, you will notice a common lingo going back and forth. (Yes there really is a Facebook group for everything.) This is done so that instead of writing several sentences describing a trade, it can be portrayed in a few lines. Here's an example from a typical Facebook post.

HD @ 333.43
STO 3 May 19, 2023 270 PUT @ 6.25 DTE 156
Collected $1,875

What this means is HD, Home Depot, was trading at $333.43 at the time of this trade. STO, sold to open, means that a credit was received. The number 3 after STO means that 3 Options were sold. The amount of the credit is $6.25 per share or $625x3 which is $1875. The Option will expire on May 19, 2023. PUTs were sold. At the time of the trade, 156 days were remaining on the contract (DTE=Days Till Expiration). Notes are sometimes entered to add context to the sentiment of the stock at that time and why. It could look like this:

HD @ 333.43
STO 3 May 19, 2023 270 PUT @ 6.25 DTE 156
Collected $1875
I think HD will move up. Interest rates have been steadying and home building appears to still be on the rise.

After a couple of months, the poster replies with the closing trade.

HD @ 338.30
STC 3 May 19, 2023 270 PUT @ 2.80 DIT 87
Profit $1035

Looking at the 2 posts, you can see that HD moved up in price by about $5. This trader bought back the 3 Options for $280 each, for a profit of $1,035. The trade was open for 87 days (DIT=Days in Trade).

Use this shorthand to log your own trades. Once you're comfortable reading and writing in this shorthand, swapping trade ideas with others will become much easier. Writing in this way will also train your brain to interpret this lingo. Just as you would with learning a new language, the more reading and writing you do in that language the faster it becomes second nature to you.

It's practice time!

The following trade is executed:
MCD @ 291.29
BTO 1 Feb 17, 2023 270 PUT @ 1.73 DTE 42
Paid $173
What is the Max Profit?
What is the Max Loss?
What is the Break Even?

Kathy is bullish on CAH. She should do the following:
1. Buy a Call
2. Buy a Put
3. Sell a Call
4. Sell a Put

The following trade is executed.
KO @ 63.67
STO 4 Jun 16, 2023 65 PUT @ 2.01 DTE 58
Collected $804
What is the Max Profit?
What is the Max Loss?
What is the Break Even?

The following trade is executed.

XOM @ 115.63

STO 1 Jun 16, 2023 125 CALL @ 1.35 DTE 57

Collected $135

What is the Max Profit?

What is the Max Loss?

What is the Break Even?

Sam is bearish on CAT. He should do the following:

1. Buy a Call

2. Buy a Put

3. Sell a Call

4. Sell a Put

The following trade is executed.

LULU @ 376.71

BTO 4 Jun 2, 2023 385 CALL @ 11.75 DTE 43

Paid $4,700

What is the Max Profit?

What is the Max Loss?

What is the Break Even?

Answers

The following trade is executed:

MCD @ 291.29

BTO 1 Feb 17, 2023 270 PUT @ 1.73 DTE 42

Paid $173

What is the Max Profit? **27,000 - 173 = $26,827**

What is the Max Loss? **$173**

What is the Break Even? **270 - 1.73 = $268.73**

Kathy is bullish on CAH. She should do the following:

*1. Buy a Call

2. Buy a Put

3. Sell a Call

*4. Sell a Put

Both Buying a Call and Selling a Put are bullish strategies.

The following trade is executed.

KO @ 63.67

STO 4 Jun 16, 2023 65 PUT @ 2.01 DTE 58

Collected $804

What is the Max Profit? **$804**

What is the Max Loss? **((65 - 2.01) * 4) * 100 = $24,920**

What is the Break Even? **65 - 2.01 = $62.30**

The following trade is executed.

XOM @ 115.63

STO 1 Jun 16, 2023 125 CALL @ 1.35 DTE 57

Collected $135

What is the Max Profit? **$135**

What is the Max Loss? **UNLIMITED**

What is the Break Even? **125 + 1.35 = $126.35**

Yes, Max Loss can be UNLIMITED!

Sam is bearish on CAT. He should do the following:

1. Buy a Call

*2. Buy a Put

*3. Sell a Call

4. Sell a Put

But remember, if Sam sells a Call without owning 100 shares of CAT, his Max Loss can be UNLIMITED. Tread carefully.

The following trade is executed.

LULU @ 376.71

BTO 4 Jun 2, 2023 385 CALL @ 11.75 DTE 43

Paid $4,700

What is the Max Profit? **UNLIMITED**

What is the Max Loss? **$4,700**

What is the Break Even? **385 + 11.75 = $396.75**

Chapter Seven

Strategies For Success

T o this point, you've learned that there are many moving parts with Options. Within the actual trade, the individual parts are known as legs. It will start to look like a game of Chicken Foot, but hang in there with me.

Understanding Legs of a Trade

Options strategies involve the choice of underlying, type, strike, expiration, and quantity. For each Option position taken, there are various risk and reward profiles. These positions are known as legs of a trade. The term legs of an Options trade is a fancy way of saying the Option position under each underlying. A trader can have one leg in a trade. Nice, clean, and neat. Once more legs are added on both sides (Calls and Puts), along with varying quantities & expirations, the risk profile of the entire trade can get quite murky. The creativity in using these legs is truly up to the trader. Luckily, a defined set of trades exists that any trader can use. No matter the experience level. Let's begin with an easy, low-risk trade, Vertical spreads.

Vertical Spreads

Vertical spreads are great for beginner Options traders. They limit risk and are IRA-friendly. Rules governing IRAs stipulate that an investor cannot sell naked Calls or Puts. Selling naked means that the trader does not have either the funds or the stock to cover the position if the Option gets assigned. And because there's limited risk, even traders with small accounts can execute vertical spreads. By setting up a vertical spread, traders are then allowed to carry those short positions because the long Option would cover the trade if the short Option got exercised. Vertical spreads have the following characteristics.

- 2 legs

- BTO 1 leg

- STO 1 leg

- Same Underlying

- Same Side (Call or Put)

- Different Strikes

- Same Expiration

There are 4 types of vertical spreads that can be executed.

1. Long Call Vertical aka **Bull Call Spread**

2. Long Put Vertical aka **Bear Put Spread**

3. Short Call Vertical aka **Bear Call Spread**

4. Short Put Vertical aka **Bull Put Spread**

The further OTM leg is referred to as the Wing. This wing is the leg that allows limited loss in the trade, making the overall trade IRA friendly.

I know at this point this is starting to look like a map out of a horror film... but now that you see the mechanics involved, the game of Chicken Foot looks way easier to play. Knowing the details of all these legs is ultimately what's going to paint clear risk for you in your trades. There is a payoff to all of this. The first two spreads are long spreads. That means the trader is paying a debit to open the trade. Let's start with a Long Call Vertical Spread.

Long Call Vertical aka Bull Call Spread

Bull Call Spread Setup

Sentiment	Bullish
Buy to Open (BTO)	1 ATM or ITM Call
Sell to Open (STO)	1 OTM Call (wing)
Expiration	Same

Bull Call Spread Profit Analysis

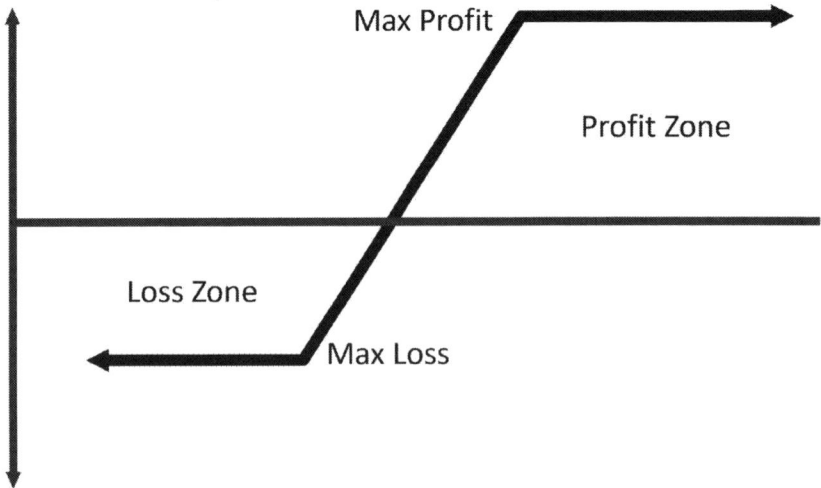

Fig 7a. Bull Call Spread Profit Analysis

With a Bull Call Spread, the trader is paying a debit when opening the trade. With opening trade debits, the stock *must* move in the correct direction to profit. In this case, the stock must rise in price.

The Max Profit, Max Loss and Break Even point are similar to calculating long Options. The difference is both profits and losses are capped. The calculations for MP, ML, and BE are as follows:

Max Profit	**(Difference Between Strikes - Debit Paid per share) x 100**
Max Loss	**Debit Paid per share x 100**
Break Even	**Long Strike + Debit Paid per share**

Example:

Martin believes that LOW is ready to move higher in the next 30 days. He buys a Bull Call Spread in LOW with 45 DTE.

Setup:
LOW @ 202.43
BTO 1 Feb 17, 2023 200 CALL @ 11.20 DTE 45
STO 1 Feb 17, 2023 210 CALL @ 6.25 DTE 45
Paid $4.95 per share

The risk associated with any vertical spread is correlated to the distance between the 2 strikes. This distance is referred to as the *width* of the spread. The wider the spread, the more risk is on the table. The tighter the width, the risk drops, but the maximum profit also drops.

Max Profit	(210 - 200 – 4.95) x 100 = $505
Max Loss	4.95 x 100 = $495
Break Even	200 + 4.95 = 204.95

In this example, Martin's trade will profit if LOW moves above $204.95 at the end of 45 days. If the trade goes against him, the most he'll lose is $495. If LOW moves above and beyond both strikes, then the max profit will be $505. Although his sentiment is that the stock will move in 30 days, he chose 45 DTE to give him some cushion in case he was wrong.

Now that we've covered Long Call Vertical Spreads, let's shift our focus to Long Put Vertical Spreads.

Long Put Vertical aka Bear Put Spread

Bear Put Spread Setup	
Sentiment	Bearish
Buy to Open (BTO)	1 ATM or ITM Put
Sell to Open (STO)	1 OTM Put (wing)
Expiration	Same

Bear Put Spread Profit Analysis

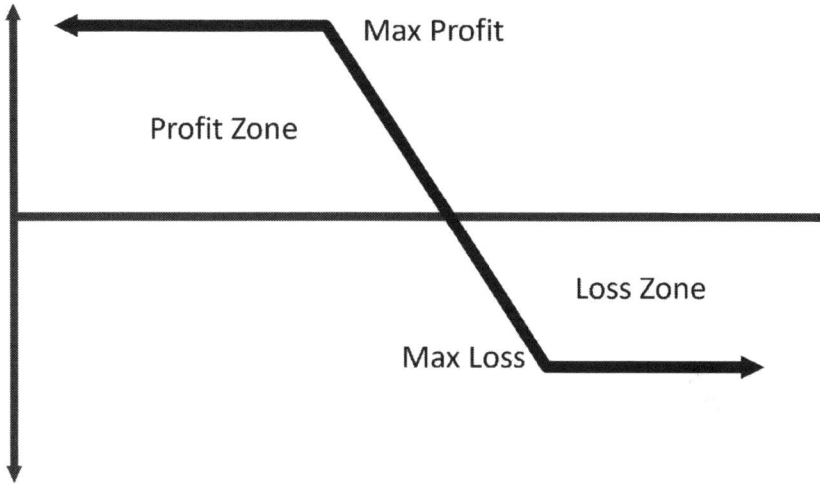

Fig 7b. Bear Put Spread Profit Analysis

As with a Bull Call Spread, a Bear Put Spread incurs paying a debit when opening the trade. With opening trade debits, the stock *must* move in the correct direction to profit. In this case, the stock must drop in price. MP, ML, and BE are as follows:

Max Profit	**(Difference Between Strikes - Debit Paid per share) x 100**
Max Loss	**Debit Paid per share x 100**
Break Even	**Long Strike - Debit Paid per share**

Example:

Bonnie believes that TGT is going to drop in the next 30 days. She buys a Bear Put Spread in TGT with 45 DTE

Setup:

TGT @ 142.30
BTO 1 Feb 17, 2023 140 PUT @ 6.10 DTE 45
STO 1 Feb 17, 2023 135 PUT @ 4.30 DTE 45
Paid $1.80 per share

Max Profit	**(140 - 135 - 1.80) x 100 = $320**
Max Loss	**1.80 x 100 = $180**
Break Even	**140 - 1.80 = $138.20**

In this example, Bonnie will profit if TGT drops below $138.20 at the end of 45 days. If the trade goes against her, the most she'll lose is $180. If TGT moves below and beyond both strikes, then the max profit will be $320. Although her sentiment is that the stock will drop in 30 days, she chose 45 DTE to give her some cushion in case she was wrong.

The Bear Put Spreads give investors, even those with small accounts, opportunities to make money in the stock market, even if the market is dropping.

Managing Long Spreads

Many Options traders close trades well before the expiration date. A common practice for long spreads is to select a percentage of the max profit to close the trade.

Example:

Louie bought a Bull Call Spread. He calculated the max profit to be $196. Louie's trading style is to sell spreads once it reaches 75% of max profit.

Knowing this, Louie sets a GTC (Good Till Cancelled) order for the entire spread to sell at $3.43. Remember, 3.43 is entered in the GTC order because Options are connected to 100 shares of stock. This number is calculated as

Max Profit Per Share x (1+% of Max Profit)

1.96 x 1.75 = $3.43

When the GTC order goes through, then Louie will have realized a profit of $147.

The percentage of MP is completely up to the trader. The higher the percentage, the longer the trader will have to wait for the GTC order to fill. Common percentages to select are between 50% - 99% of max profit. The lower the percentage, the smaller the amount of profit, but the chances of that hitting are greater. If the trade is nearing expiration and it still hasn't closed, the chances of it hitting decrease due to Theta decay. The choice at this point is to let the trade expire worthless or sell it before expiration just to get some money back. Since this is a limited-risk trade, most traders accept the max loss and move on.

Lastly, long spreads should be closed before expiration. If a trader leaves the position through expiration, even if both legs are ITM, there is an extra hassle to close the positions after the fact.

To paint a clear picture for you, consider these scenarios.

Eric holds a long call spread in AAPL. He forgets about expiration and the long call expires ITM while the short call expires worthless. Come Monday morning, Eric will find 100 shares of AAPL in his account. He may not have wanted this, but now he's stuck with the shares.

What if both short and long legs expired ITM? Then the broker will auto-exercise both positions. Since they cancel each other out, no positions will be left in Eric's account on Monday. But he may have incurred assignment fees. Some brokers charge $10 per assignment. In Eric's case, two legs, two assignments, with $20 extra in fees. The point is - as a beginner, close your spreads before expiration. Eric clearly learned a lesson here. With more experience and knowledge, holding positions through expiration days will get less stressful.

Some brokers charge zero assignment fees, so this scenario may not apply.

Having covered Long Vertical Spreads, let's now take a 180 turn and focus on Short Vertical Spreads. We'll explore the distinct characteristics and qualities that set them apart.

Short Call Vertical aka Bear Call Spread

Bear Call Spread Setup	
Sentiment	Bearish
Sell to Open (STO)	1 ATM or ITM Call
Buy to Open (BTO)	1 OTM Call (wing)
Expiration	Same

Bear Call Spread Profit Analysis

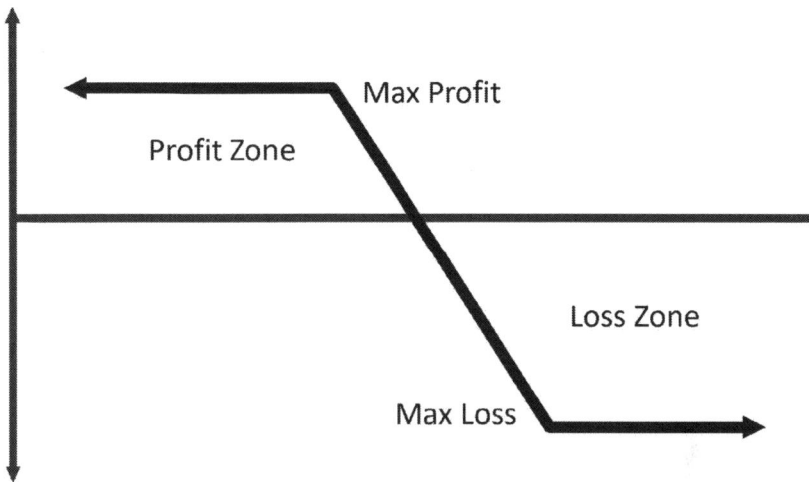

Fig 7c. Bear Call Spread Profit Analysis

With a Bear Call Spread, the trader is receiving a credit when opening the trade. With opening trade credits, the stock could either move in the correct direction or stay the same for the trader to make a profit. In this case, the stock must either stay the same or move down in price. Calculations shown as:

Max Profit	**Credit Received per share x 100**
Max Loss	**(Difference Between Strikes - Credit Received per share) x 100**
Break Even	**Short Strike + Credit Received per share**

For Example:

Jack believes that PEP is going to drop in the next 30 days. He sells a Bear Call Spread in PEP with 45 DTE

Setup:

PEP @ 182.50
STO 1 Feb 17, 2023 185 PUT @ 4.75 DTE 45
BTO 1 Feb 17, 2023 190 PUT @ 2.63 DTE 45
Received $2.12 per share

Max Profit	**2.12 x 100 = $212**
Max Loss	**(190 - 185 - 2.12) x 100 = $288**
Break Even	**185 + 2.12 = $187.12**

In this example, Jack will profit if PEP stays below $187.12 at the end of 45 days. If the trade goes against him, the most he'll lose is $288. If PEP moves below and beyond both strikes, then the max profit will be $212. Although his sentiment is that the stock will drop in 30 days, he chose 45 DTE to give him some cushion in case he was wrong. The value of a Bear Call Spread is that you can short a stock (bet that it will go lower) in a limited account or IRA. Shorting straight stock requires a margin account. Using Bear Call Spreads allows investors to make money, even when the market is going down. Remember our analogy about betting on a team everyone knows is going to lose... Bear Call spreads allow you to make money on a losing team, or market that is going down.

Okay, time for our final vertical spread: the Bull Put Spread.

Short Put Vertical aka Bull Put Spread

Bull Put Spread Setup	
Sentiment	Bullish
Sell to Open (STO)	1 ATM or ITM Put
Buy to Open (BTO)	1 OTM Put (wing)
Expiration	Same

Bull Put Spread Profit Analysis

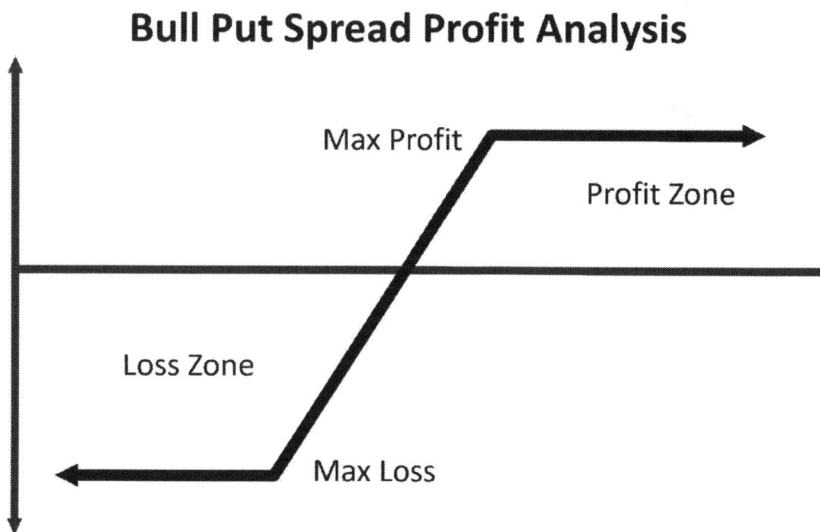

Fig 7d. Bull Put Spread Profit Analysis

With a Bull Put Spread, the trader is receiving a credit when opening the trade. With opening trade credits, the stock could either move in the correct direction or stay the same for the trader to make a profit. In this case, the stock must either stay the same or move up in price.

Max Profit	Credit Received per share x 100
Max Loss	(Difference Between Strikes - Credit Received per share) x 100
Break Even	Short Strike - Credit Received per share

For Example:

Phoebe believes that T is going to rise in the next 30 days. She sells a Bull Put Spread in T with 45 DTE

Setup:

T @ 18.27
STO 1 Feb 17, 2023 18 PUT @ .65 DTE 45
BTO 1 Feb 17, 2023 13 PUT @ .3 DTE 45
Received $.35 per share

Max Profit	.35 x 100 = $35
Max Loss	(18 - 13 - .35) x 100 = $465
Break Even	18 - .35 = $17.65

In this example, Phoebe will profit if T stays above $17.65 at the end of 45 days. If the trade goes against her, the most she'll lose is $465. If T stays above and beyond both strikes, then the max profit will be $35. Although her sentiment is that the stock will rise in 30 days, she chose 45 DTE to give her some cushion in case she was wrong as the loss far outweighs what the profit could be.

Managing Short Spreads

As with long spreads, many Options traders close short trades well before the expiration date. A common practice for short-spread management is to select a percentage of the max profit to close the trade. With short verticals, the max profit is the amount of premium collected.

For Example:

Cecilia sold a Bull Put Spread for $204. Cecilia's trading style is to buy spreads back once it reaches 50% of the premium collected. Knowing this, Cecilia sets a GTC (Good Till Cancelled) order to buy back the entire spread at $1.02. This number is calculated as:

Premium Collected Per Share x (1-% of premium collected)

2.04 x .5 = $1.02

When the GTC order goes through, then Cecilia will have realized a profit of $102 or 50% of Max Profit.

Again, the percentage of MP is completely up to the trader. The higher the percentage, the longer the trader will have to wait for the GTC order to fill. Common percentages to select are between 25% - 75% of MP. The lower the percentage, the smaller the amount of profit, but the chances of that hitting are greater. As with long spreads, traders should close positions before expiration. Keeping positions open isn't worth the stress and hassle of assignment. The major difference between short spreads versus long spreads is the choice to let the positions expire worthless. If a short trader is correct and the two legs move further OTM, nothing needs to be done. The legs will expire worthless and max profit is achieved.

Vertical Options spreads are great because you don't need to own any stocks to trade. Predict the stock's likely direction and enjoy limited risk. It's a beginner-friendly choice. Vertical spreads reduce the chance of losing all your money in one trade.

Limited Risk Neutral Strategies – Iron Condor and Iron Butterfly

What do you think will happen when we combine two vertical spreads? Well, now it's getting fun. You'll be getting double benefits on both sides of the trade. Let's start with Iron Condors. Yep, the profit analysis of an Iron Condor kind of looks like a flapping bird.

Iron Condor

The construction of an Iron Condor is the combination of an OTM Bear Call Spread and an OTM Bull Put Spread.

Iron Condor Setup

Sentiment	Neutral
Sell to Open (STO)	1 OTM Bear Call Spread
Sell to Open (STO)	1 OTM Bull Put Spread
Expiration	Same
Note	Bear Call and Bull Put Have Same Width

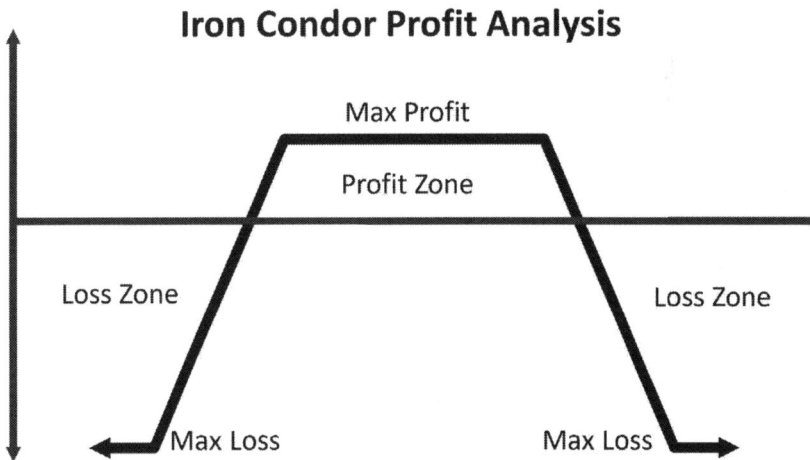

Iron Condor Profit Analysis

Max Profit

Profit Zone

Loss Zone

Loss Zone

Max Loss

Max Loss

Fig 7e. Iron Condor Profit Analysis

The key benefits of this trade are that it's neutral and has limited risk. Iron condors are basically creating a profit range where the current price of the stock lies between the 2 short legs. The distance between the two short legs is the width of the condor. The wider the width, the more chance of profit, but that maximum profit is reduced. The narrower the width, the less chance of profit, but the max profit is increased. The distance of the wings also affects the trade. The further out the wings are, the higher the max profit. With further out wings, the amount of risk goes up. Traders use iron condors like a shotgun with birdshot. With a shotgun, you have the birdshot that is widespread so you don't have to be dead center on your target. Whereas with other guns or with a bow and arrow you have to be dead on to hit your target. This is the case with Iron condors, instead of aiming for an exact price at expiration, the trader just needs to hit within a range. This allows some movement up or down. The goal of an iron condor is for the price to stay within range and with patience, Theta will decay the short positions into profitability. Bear Call Spreads and Put Bull Spreads both collect premiums. These 2 premiums combined are the max profit for the trade.

Max Profit	**Total Credit Received per share x 100**
Max Loss on Call Side	**(Difference Between Strikes - Total Credit Received per share) x 100**
Max Loss on Put Side	**(Difference Between Strikes - Total Credit Received per share) x 100**
Break Even on Call Side	**Short Strike + Total Credit Received per share**
Break Even on Put Side	**Short Strike - Total Credit Received per share**

Here's an example.

Tony's research tells him that WMT will stay within a range in the next 30 days. WMT is currently at $141.79. He sets up an iron condor.

Bull Put Spread
STO 1 Feb 17, 2023 135 PUT @ 2.51 DTE 45
BTO 1 Feb 17, 2023 130 PUT @ 1.56 DTE 45
Received $.95 per share

+

Bear Call Spread
STO 1 Feb 17, 2023 150 CALL @ 1.81 DTE 45
BTO 1 Feb 17, 2023 155 CALL @ .75 DTE 45
Received $1.06 per share

Total Credit Received $2.01

Max Profit	2.01 x 100 = $201
Max Loss on Call Side	(155 - 150 - 2.01) x 100 = $299
Max Loss on Put Side	(135 - 130 - 2.01) x 100 = $299
Break Even on Call Side	150 + 2.01 = $152.01
Break Even on Put Side	135 - 2.01 = $127.99

In this example, Tony will profit if WMT stays between $127.99 and $152.01 at the end of 45 days. If the trade goes against him, the most he'll lose is $299. If WMT stays between $130 and $150, his max profit will be $201. Although his sentiment is that the stock will stay range bound in 30 days, he chose 45 DTE to give him some cushion in case he was wrong.

With this example, the amount of maximum profit is increased vs single vertical spreads. This is because premiums are added on both sides of the Options table. With increased premiums received, the range of profits increases.

Managing Iron Condors

A common practice to manage iron condors is to close the trade once it hits 50% of the max profit. In the example above, Tony would set a GTC buy order to close the entire position at $1.00. The expiration is 45 days. Using the technique in Chapter 5 to predict the future, if the stock doesn't move, Tony's GTC order should trigger in 30 days.

Taking profits at 50% of max profit is a common rule, but of course, it depends on the trader. The higher the number, the longer the trade will last. The lower the number, the chances of closing for a profit increase, but that dollar amount will be smaller. For traders that like to go in and out of trades, they make that percentage smaller. More patient traders increase that percentage.

Now, what happens when the short Put and Call fall on the same strike? You get an Iron Butterfly. No, I'm not making up these names.

Iron Butterfly

Iron Butterflies and Iron Condors are alike in one regard - they both combine a Bear Call Spread and a Bull Put Spread. However, the difference is the short Call and the short Put land on the same strike.

Iron Butterfly Setup	
Sentiment	Neutral
Sell to Open (STO)	1 ATM Bear Call Spread
Sell to Open (STO)	1 ATM Bull Put Spread
Expiration	Same
Note	Bear Call and Bull Put Have Same Width and Both Short Options Land on the Same Strike

Iron Butterfly Profit Analysis

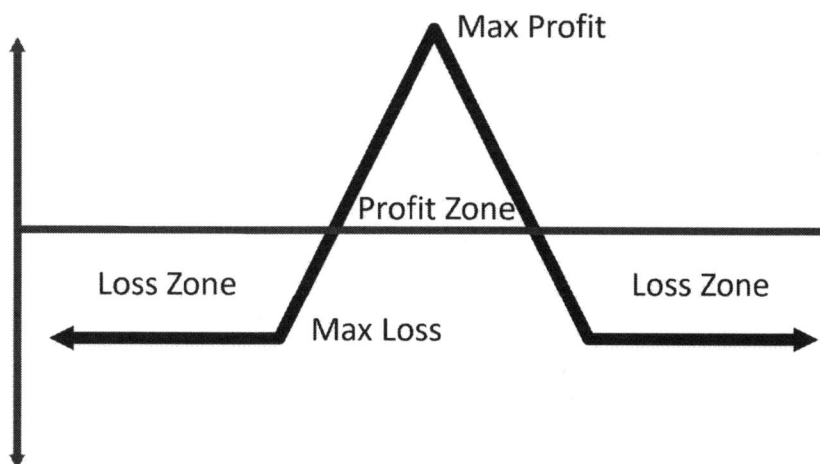

Fig 7f. Iron Butterfly Profit Analysis

The key benefits of this trade are that it's both neutral and carries limited risk. Iron Butterflies are basically Iron Condors, but the 2 short legs are on the same strike. An Iron Butterfly is a popular tool for earnings trades. With earnings trades, Vega is high. Once the earnings report is over, Vega drops. If the trader believes the earnings report will be *normal*, then the price of the stock shouldn't move much. If he is right, then when Vega drops, he can buy back the Options at a lower price.

Remember the shotgun analogy? Well, Iron Butterflies are also like a shotgun with birdshot. The difference is the range is much tighter. This allows some movement up or down, but not much as with the Iron Condor. Bear Call Spreads and Put Bull Spreads both collect premiums. These 2 premiums combined are the max profit for the trade.

Here's an example.

Sandy's research tells her that ABBV will stay within range through earnings. ABBV is currently at $158.05. She sets up an Iron Butterfly.

Bull Put Spread
STO 1 Feb 17, 2023 160 PUT @ 6.80 DTE 45
BTO 1 Feb 17, 2023 150 PUT @ 2.92 DTE 45
Received $3.88

+

Bear Call Spread
STO 1 Feb 17, 2023 160 CALL @ 4.45 DTE 45
BTO 1 Feb 17, 2023 170 CALL @ 1.20 DTE 45
Received $3.25 per share

Total Credit Received $7.13

Max Profit	7.13 x 100 = $713
Max Loss on Call Side	(170 - 160 - 7.13) x 100 = $287
Max Loss on Put Side	(160 - 150 - 7.13) x 100 = $287
Break Even on Call Side	160 + 7.13 = $167.13
Break Even on Put Side	160 − 7.13 = $152.87

In this example, Sandy will profit if ABBV stays between $152.87 and $167.13 at the end of 45 days. If the trade goes against her, the most she'll lose is $287. If ABBV lands exactly on $160 at expiration, her max profit will be $713.

Managing Iron Butterflies

The common practice to manage Iron Butterflies is to close the trade once it hits 25% of the max profit. In the example above, Sandy would set a GTC buy order to close the entire position at $5.34. The total profit will be $179. The 25% is a common rule, but of course, depends on the trader.

Iron Condors and Iron Butterflies are credit spreads, meaning you collect cash when you start the trade. You can also buy Iron Condors and Iron Butterflies. But those trades depend on large swings in stock price to be profitable. I'm not saying those are bad trades. It's just harder to predict the direction *and* velocity of the underlying's price. Go ahead and experiment with these spreads. Play around like a scientist in the stock market laboratory and discover what combinations work best for you and the stocks you want to trade. Remember, we all develop our own style of trading. Through time, you'll find your winning formula.

Alright, let's imagine you're not into all that fancy day trading or swing trading stuff. Don't worry, I've got a strategy for you that's perfect for the lazy but effective investor in you. It's called "The Wheel." Just like a hamster running in circles, this strategy will help you invest and grow your money while putting in minimal effort.

The Wheel

The wheel strategy is a combination of two strategies repeated through time. This strategy is quite popular with beginners **and** experienced traders alike because it's relatively simple yet yields impressive results over a long period of time. Because it is a long-term process, there are steps to follow. Let's go over them.

Sell Put (Cash Secured Put - CSP)

➤ Sell Put

➤ Put Stock

➤ Sell Call (Covered Call)

➤ Sell Call

Steps of a Wheel

➤ Stock Called Away

➤ Repeat

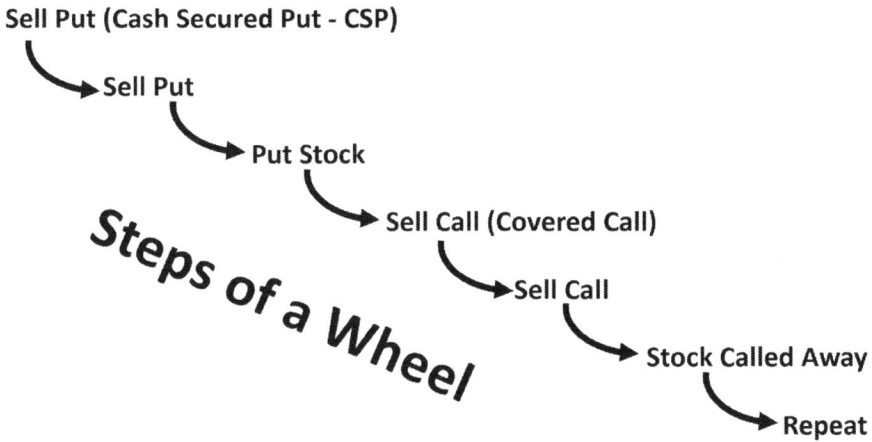

Fig 7g. Steps of a Wheel

Step 1 – Sell Put aka Cash Secured Put

The first step is selling an OTM Put in a stock that you want to own. The last part of that sentence is the most important. "That you want to own." Before we dive in, let's make sure you're mentally prepared for the long haul. This strategy is all about committing to holding onto a stock for years or even decades. So, strap on your investing helmet and get ready for an endurance race. Placing a short put on a stock means that you are willing to own 100 shares of said stock at the strike price. Working with high-priced stocks can leave you with a cash requirement in the 10's of thousands of dollars. Be prepared emotionally and financially to take on that risk. Once you've made your choice on underlying, select an expiry of about 45-60 DTE. This will give you a good amount of premium for the trade. Then select a strike that you're willing to hold the stock.

Here's an example:

Wendy has $10,000 in her trading account. After some research, she decides that she wants to own 100 shares of SCHD. SCHD is currently trading at $76.19. She sells an OTM put at strike 75, 45 DTE for $1.17. If SCHD stays above 75 at expiration, then she keeps the $117. She can then repeat step 1. If SCHD drops below $75 at expiration, she will be Put the stock at $75 per share. The following Monday, she'll own 100 shares of SCHD costing $7,500. She also keeps the $117 premium she collected at the beginning of the trade. At this point, she moves on to Step 2.

Step 2 – Sell Call aka Covered Call

If a trader owns 100 shares of a stock, then they can sell a Call against those shares. A Covered Call is offering your owned stock for sale at a certain strike price. In a short Put, the risk is cash. In a short Call, the risk is shares of stock. In using shares as risk, a trader is capping the upside of the shares. In selecting the strikes for the Call, make sure you are comfortable with selling the shares at the strike price. Selecting a Call strike that's low will give you good premium, but will give you fewer gains if the shares are called away. To determine a good Call strike, calculate the cost basis for the entire trade. This is done by adding all of the credits and subtracting all of the debits from the beginning of the wheel. This will give you the true cost of the 100 shared owned.

Let's go back to the previous example.

Wendy bought 100 shares of SCHD for $7500. Since she sold a put 45 days earlier, she collected $117. This means that the true cost, or cost basis, of those 100 shares is $7,383. If she decides to sell a Call, she should make sure that the strike selected plus the premium will be equal to or more than $73.83. That way she ensures she at least breaks even in the transaction.

Here's an example of hypothetical trades that Wendy may go through that contribute to cost basis.

1/1/2023 Sell 75 Put for $117
1/30/2023 Put Expires Worthless, Keep $117
2/1/2023 Sell 75 Put $115

2/28/2023 Stock Drops, Put stock for $7,500

3/1/2023 Sell 80 Call for $60

3/30/2023 Call Expires Worthless, Keep $60

4/1/2023 Sell 80 Call for $65

Cost basis calculation: 117 + 115 - 7500 + 60 + 65 = -$7,143 ($71.43 per share)

4/30/2023 Stock Rises Above $80, Shares Called Away at $80 per share

After the shares get called away at $80 per share, Wendy will have a profit of $857. If she didn't sell any Options and purchased the stock at $76.19, her profit would be $381. She would have missed out on an extra $476 of free money.

Selling Covered Calls is a great way of getting extra income from owned stocks. When you own stocks, you can make money when the price of the stock rises above your buy price. But, did you actually make money that you can spend to buy groceries? Not yet. Those are paper profits. To make money that you can actually spend, you must either wait for any dividends (if any) or sell some shares and use the profits to make your purchases. When investing using the Wheel strategy, you can make extra cash with the Call premiums you sell. This is a way of turning your shares of stock into a "rental property." With rental properties, you are invested in them for the long-term profit - so is the case with the wheel strategy.

Monitoring a Wheel's cost basis is key to decision-making when selecting strikes. Do not select Call strikes that you are not comfortable losing your shares at. Make sure that the strike you select plus any premiums are higher than your cost basis. Of course, there may be times when you feel like getting out of the trade completely. Let's say the stock took a turn for the worse and is now trading well below your cost basis. The premiums that you could be collecting around your cost basis are so small that it makes it not worth it. A couple of things you can do.

1. Stay patient and wait until the stock recovers then start selling calls again. Remember, you'll be collecting dividends throughout this process, further bringing your cost basis down.

2. Sell a call below your cost basis. Make sure you are completely comfortable with taking a loss if the stock gets called away at that price.

Know the risk of running a wheel. When selling below cost basis, the risk is locking in your losses for the entire trade. When selling above cost basis, the risk is the opportunity cost if the stock rockets above the Call strike.

I once talked with a trader that had a wheel going with Tesla. Now Tesla is what you call a high flyer. The price swings in this stock are so great that premiums are always pushed very high. This trader owned 2,000 shares of Tesla. Her cost basis was about $200 per share for a total of $400,000. But the stock dropped down to $150, well below $200. Her account is now $300,000 for a paper loss of $100,000. She freaked out and tried to get some money back by selling Calls against those shares. The strike she chose was $170. Then what happened? You guessed it. TSLA rockets up and blows past $170. Now she's freaking out again because if her shares get called away, she locks in about a $60,000 loss. Not good. Ultimately, she sold all her positions, took the loss, and swore off Options for the rest of her life. Don't be like her... you have the knowledge now to avoid the scenario she found herself in.

The lesson of this story? Choose underlyings and strikes wisely. Is Tesla a good trading vehicle? Sure. Did she want to own the stock for years, decades, or generations? Probably not. Did she choose strikes wisely? Nope.

A little management strategy that may have helped her, in this case, is Rolling Positions.

Rolling Positions

Rolling positions is essentially a defensive move when Options trades go wrong. This process involves closing the current (usually losing trade) and re-establishing using longer-term expirations. This is known as Rolling Out. Rolling is only advantageous to Options sellers. This is because selling Options further into the future yields more collected premiums (Theta). The more premiums collected, the higher the chance of profit. Rolling also allows short sellers to reestablish strikes further away from ATM to protect against assignment. This is referred to as either rolling up or rolling down. If your new strike is priced higher than your old strike, then you're rolling up. If your new strike is priced lower than your old strike, then you're rolling down. In the case of the Tesla trader, she should have rolled her position further out into the future and rolled it up to a higher strike. She may have to pay a small debit for the roll, but it will save her as the stock stabilizes and/or drops a little. After several rolls, she may decide to give up her shares. By rolling up, she'll be able to sell those shares at a higher price.

There are two basic rules for rolling as a short seller. 1) Try to collect a credit for each roll. 2) Try to move the short strike further away from ITM. You'll be in good shape if you can achieve these with each roll. Stocks tend to stabilize after big moves. Rolling will keep you afloat as you wait for things to cool down.

Rolling typically does not work well for defined risk trades like Iron Condors or Vertical Spreads. The cost of the further legs eats at the incoming premiums. This makes it harder to collect a credit for each roll.

Options buyers can also roll positions, but the chances of profit decrease because they are paying for the opportunity to be directionally right.

Finally, you may be wondering *when* to roll. Here's a tip. If you hold a short position that's deep ITM, wait until the extrinsic value is close to zero. This may take you all the way to expiration day, down to the last minutes. As a beginner, this may cause you great stress. If your stress level is too high, roll sooner. Nothing wrong with that. And always remember to think about dividend risk if you hold short calls. With more experience, you'll get used to holding these "dangerous" positions during expiration days. As short sellers, we collect premium in the beginning of the trade. We're receiving the extrinsic value that the holder paid for. As the Option decays, the extrinsic value goes into your account. You're basically squeezing as much extrinsic value as you can before you roll.

I've spoken several times in this book regarding thinking in the long term. Options trades are meant to be short-term trades. But you will come across losers here and there. Rolling losing trades out into the future extends the trade, turning your short-term trade into a long-term trade. No limit exists on how long you want to keep a trade going. You can literally roll and roll and roll. Eventually, you'll either break even, take a smaller loss vs not rolling, or make a profit.

If you're looking to supercharge your Wheel, the next strategy is a surefire way to do it – by adding more risk. You might be wondering, isn't adding risk dangerous? Well, not necessarily. Let's take a deep dive into the Covered Strangle.

Covered Strangle or Short Strangle

The Wheel is a very effective tool to maximize profits. Now you can take the Wheel to the next level. The following strategy offers high reward possibilities. But it does come with higher risk. This is because they require the trader to have risk on both the Put and the Call side. This is a Covered Strangle or Short Strangle.

Let's go back to Investing 101. The basic premise is to continuously squirrel away a little bit of extra cash into an investment vehicle like stocks. The more frequently you do this, the faster your investment account grows. While investing in Options, this saving of money shouldn't stop. Smart investors are constantly putting money away, usually in an automated fashion.

Now, consider you've been in a Wheel trade for several months. During that time, you've collected premiums, collected dividends, and made cash deposits. You now have enough cash to buy 100 more shares of your Wheeled stock. This is where the rules of selecting underlyings are very important. More specifically, is the stock you're buying one that you want to own for years, decades, or generations? If that's true, then you would love to purchase more if you have enough cash. Using a Covered Strangle is the way.

A Covered Strangle is just like an Iron Condor, except it has no wings. It consists of selling 1 OTM Call and selling 1 OTM Put. This has more reward than Iron Condors because you don't have to buy the wings. You are collecting premiums on both sides of the trade without paying extra for the further-out Options. This gives you more chances of profit. But, max loss is "infinite" both ways if the stock moves beyond the Call or the Put strikes. But is the loss really infinite? If a Covered Strangle went against you on the Put side, you'd end up with more stock you wanted anyway. If the Strangle went against you on the Call side, you'll end up selling your shares at a higher price than you purchased them. Either way, sounds good to me.

Comparison of Covered Strangle and Iron Condor

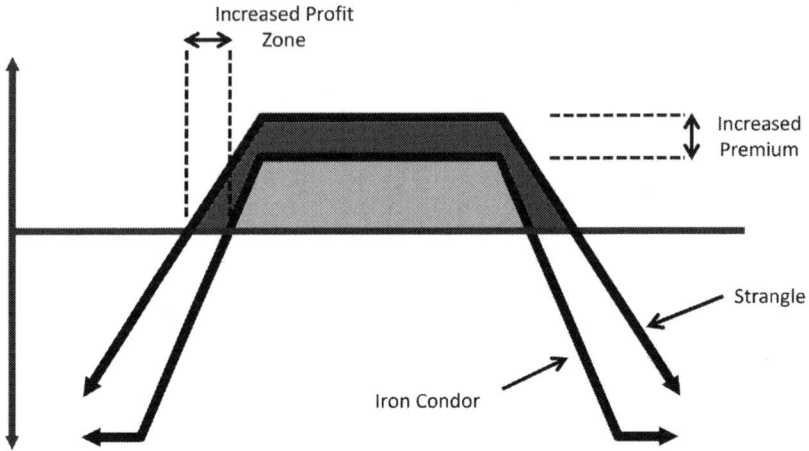

Fig 7h. Covered Strangle and Iron Condor Comparison

Investing is a long-term endeavor. Successful entrepreneurs who invest in real estate, stocks, or businesses (no, not day trading) have one thing in common. They accumulate assets. The more assets accumulated, the more future profits. Start with the Wheel, then onto Covered Strangles...asset accumulation will become automatic. The sequence of events could now look like this.

Deposit funds until enough to buy 100 shares

Sell Put (Cash Secured Put - CSP)

Put expires worthless, keep premium

Deposit additional funds

Sell Put

Stock drops, Put 100 shares of Stock

Deposit additional funds

Sell Call (Covered Call)

Collect Dividend off 100 shares

Call expires worthless, keep premium

Deposit additional funds

Sell Call (Covered Call)

Collect Dividend off 100 shares

Call expires worthless, keep premium

Deposit additional funds

Funds now enough to purchase 100 more shares

Sell Call (Covered Call) and Cash Secured Put...Covered Strangle

Collect Dividend off 100 shares

Call and Put expires worthless, keep premium from both Call and Put

Deposit additional funds

Sell Covered Strangle

Stock drops, Put 100 shares of stock

Sell 2 Calls

Collect Dividend off 200 shares

Calls expire worthless, keep premium

Deposit additional funds

Funds now enough to purchase 100 more shares

...

Stock Called Away

Repeat

Smart underlying selection and strike selection will make this Wheel "spin." The simple rules for running a Wheel with a Covered Strangle.

1. Select Underlyings that are consistently trending upward. Guess what? Index funds like SPY historically do this ;)

2. Sell OTM Cash Secured Puts at a strike price you can afford if the stocks are put to you.

3. Sell OTM Calls above your cost basis.

4. Continuously deposit funds for investment.

Selling premium in a Wheel accomplishes three things. It gives you extra income from Options premiums. It forces you to buy stocks at a discount. And it forces you to sell stocks for higher gains. Rinse and repeat.

Now that you understand how to begin a Vertical Spread, Iron Condor, or Wheel strategy, it's important to determine the suitable strikes and expirations. What factors do Options traders consider when establishing the initial trade? Let's explore their thinking process.

Thought Process

The strategies I laid out are mainly *selling* strategies. You may have already deduced the cause...Selling Options as an opening transaction gives the trader a higher chance of profit. This is because of Option's tendency to be overpriced due to fear. Options sellers capitalize on this fear and profit as fear (Vega) & time (Theta) diminish. Selling also allows traders to profit if the stock prices don't move by expiration. And if the trade goes awry, rolling into the future can help recover and bring everything back to break even or close to break even.

The thought process for sellers is this. We want the stock price to stay within a certain range. There are a couple of tricks to determine an acceptable range. Luckily, all you have to do is look at an Option chain. Some platforms explicitly show the expected range directly in the chain. Below is an example from the Tastyworks platform.

| | MCD | IV RANK 98.4 | LAST 254.73 | CHG -3.38 | BID 252.73 | ASK 257.23 | Expected Range |

| ASSET TYPE | | TRADE MODE | STRIKES | STRATEGY | | | |
| Options | Single | Table | ALL | Vertical | Short | Put | |

OPEN I...	EXT	BID	ASK	STRIKES	BID	ASK	EXT	OPEN I...
Dec 15, 2023			CALLS	53d	PUTS			IV: 24.1% (±13.92)
3	2.51	31.70	33.00	225	1.40	1.50	1.45	2.12K
19	2.67	27.35	27.95	230	1.82	1.93	1.87	426
19	2.99	22.70	23.25	235	2.35	2.51	2.43	216
50	3.87	18.70	19.00	240	3.25	3.40	3.32	1.96K
249	4.97	14.80	15.10	245	4.35	4.55	4.45	463
901	6.39	11.30	11.45	250	5.85	6.10	5.97	731
2.61K	8.30	8.20	8.40	255	7.90	8.05	7.96	793
694	5.75	5.70	5.80	260	10.45	10.65	5.53	393
680	3.82	3.75	3.90	265	13.60	13.75	3.65	917
1.37K	2.45	2.41	2.48	270	17.25	17.60	2.40	422
492	1.53	1.47	1.59	275	21.35	22.05	1.68	431
588	0.95	0.89	1.00	280	25.35	26.65	0.98	532
691	0.59	0.52	0.67	285	30.25	31.30	0.75	265
964	0.39	0.34	0.44	290	34.70	36.20	0.43	306
784	0.24	0.17	0.32	295	39.60	41.20	0.38	72

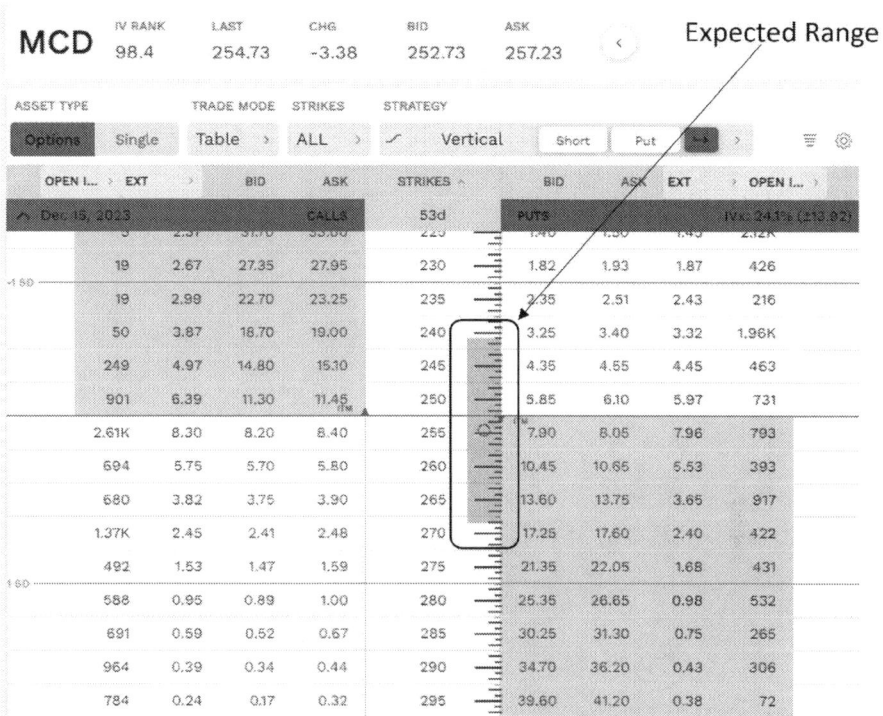

Fig 7i. Expected Range

The expected range is highlighted at the center of the chain. Based on the current market conditions, the computer system calculates the stock movement within the number of days until expiration. In this case, the stock price should stay between $240ish and $268ish. If your platform doesn't show this range, you can mimic it by placing an ATM Straddle trade. A Straddle is similar to a Strangle, but the short Put and Call are on the same strike. Here's an example.

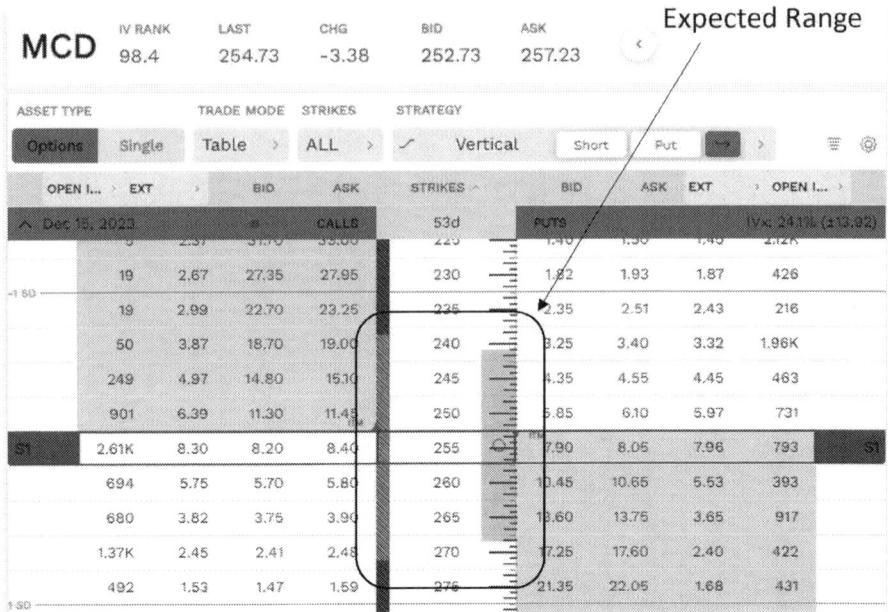

Fig 7j. Expected Range with Straddle

The range on the left signifies the profit range of the Straddle. You'll notice those two ranges are very similar to each other. Use those guides to help determine where you enter your trades.

Also, look at the extrinsic value of the Options to see if the trade is worth it. Most platforms will allow you to show the extrinsic value within the chain.

MCD	IV RANK 98.4	LAST 254.73	CHG -3.38	BID 252.73	ASK 257.23	‹	Extrinsic Value

ASSET TYPE   TRADE MODE   STRIKES   STRATEGY

Options	Single	Table ›	ALL ›	↗	Vertical	Short	Put	↦		▼ ≪

OPEN I... ›	EXT ›	BID	ASK	STRIKES ⌃		BID	ASK	EXT	› OPEN I... ›
⌃ Dec 15, 2023			CALLS	53d	PUTS				IVx: 24.1% (±13.9)
8	1.64	45.90	47.35	210		0.72	0.78	0.75	75
4	1.79	41.30	42.25	215		0.87	0.94	0.90	191
8	1.94	36.40	37.45	220		1.09	1.18	1.13	354
5	2.37	31.70	33.00	225		1.40	1.50	1.45	2.12K
19	2.67	27.35	27.95	230		1.82	1.93	1.87	426
19	2.99	22.70	23.25	235		2.35	2.51	2.43	216
50	3.87	18.70	19.00	240		3.25	3.40	3.32	1.96K
249	4.97	14.80	15.10	245		4.35	4.55	4.45	463
901	6.39	11.30	11.45	250		5.85	6.10	5.97	731
2.61K	8.30	8.20	8.40	255		7.90	8.05	7.96	793
694	5.75	5.70	5.80	260		10.45	10.65	5.53	393
680	3.82	3.75	3.90	265		13.60	13.75	3.65	917
1.37K	2.45	2.41	2.48	270		17.25	17.60	2.40	422
492	1.53	1.47	1.59	275		21.35	22.05	1.68	431
588	0.95	0.89	1.00	280		25.35	26.65	0.98	532

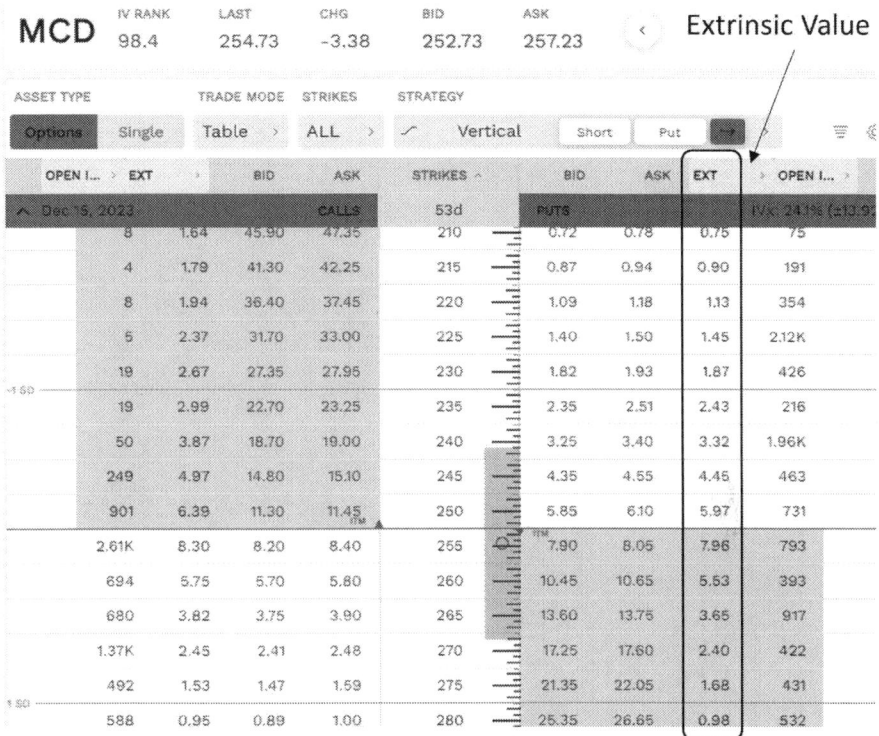

Fig 7k. Extrinsic Value

Once the extrinsic value is shown, look closer at each value. Say you're considering selling a CSP (Cash Secured Put or Short Put) in MCD. As a seller, you want your short Option to stay away from the expected range. You're considering selling at strike 235 because it's out of the range. Look at the extrinsic value and determine if the amount you'll receive is worth the trade.

37.45	220		1.09	1.18	1.13	354
33.00	225		1.40	1.50	1.45	2.12K
27.95	230		1.82	1.93	1.87	426
23.25	235		2.35	2.51	2.43	216
19.00	240		3.25	3.40	3.32	1.96K
15.10	245		4.35	4.55	4.45	463
11.45 ITM	250		5.85	6.10	5.97	731
8.40	255	ITM	7.90	8.05	7.96	793
5.80	260		10.45	10.65	5.53	393
3.90	265		13.60	13.75	3.65	917

Fig 71. Extrinsic Value Selection

The amount of extrinsic value is 2.43. This means that you will be receiving $243 if you sold the 235 Put. Is $243 worth your risk of $23,500? Maybe. Let's do some quick math. There are 53 days left for this Option. Theoretically, you could make this trade approximately 6 to 7 times throughout the year.

Days in Year / Days in Trade
365 / 53 = 6.89

The percentage payoff for this 53 day trade is

(Premium / Risk) * Number of Trades

243 / 23500 = .0103

.0103 * 6.89 = .0712

Converted into percentage = approx 7.12%

This means you can potentially make a 7% return annually with stocks you never owned. Is a 7% return worth it? It's your call.

Take note of the extrinsic value as you go further ITM and OTM. You'll notice that the further you go away from ATM, the smaller the extrinsic value gets. This means you'll make the most returns in relation to risk the closer you get to ATM.

Expiration selection is also key. As a rule, many traders open positions with more than ~30 DTE. This gives a cushion to be directionally correct. Many consider anything less than 30 gambling. But each trader develops their own style. Some traders even buy and sell 0 DTE Options with great success. That could be your cup of tea if you enjoy watching tickers all day. You'll find your own style the more you make trades. When I first started selling Cash Secured Puts, I sold OTM Puts 120 days out or more. This gave me solid premium and a lot of leeway if I was wrong. It took more patience, but it made me comfortable selling Options.

Finally, you must also look at any upcoming earnings calls and ex-dividend dates. Those two events will affect your trade decisions. Here's an example.

Fig 7m. Earnings and Ex-Dividend Date

This platform shows those dates right in the chain. If your platform does not show this, look up the information from sites like finance.yahoo.com and note when those dates are before you execute any trade. If you want to avoid those events, select expirations *before* those dates. When working with stocks that offer dividends, the earnings date is before the ex-dividend date. Typically, a couple of weeks. ETFs don't have earnings dates. They only have ex-dividend dates.

Watching the market over time will help you find trends. You'll start to notice if a stock is consistently blowing through an expected range. You'll notice that certain stocks have a habit of missing earnings, dropping, but recovering soon after. You'll notice that certain ETFs react more to world events vs other ETFs. These observations are invaluable. As you grow as a trader, your evolving market observations and newfound Options trading skills will enhance your profitability.

****

On the flip side, what if you are a seasoned stock trader and would like to capitalize on your knowledge of stock movements by buying Options? As an Option buyer, the amount of extrinsic value is the price you pay for the opportunity to be correct. Suppose you believe MCD will increase from its current price of $254.73, so you buy an ITM Call strike at 235. The extrinsic value for that Call Option is 2.99. That means you're paying an extra $299 for the opportunity to own 100 shares of MCD for 235 per share (a discount from the current price). The actual premium you're paying will be approximately $2,297, depending on the fill price. If MCD moves up $5, then the Call Option at 235 will move up approximately $4 (1 STD has an approximate Delta of .8). That means your $2,297 investment will move up to $2,697 for a 17% increase. Nice. But what if you're wrong and the stock drops to 240? In this case, you can exercise your Option, give up the $2,297 you paid, and own 100 shares of MCD at 235 per share, which is still a discount from 240. Then, you can start running the wheel. This is the reason why I started this scenario by buying a deep ITM

Call Option. Buying OTM Options is basically gambling. They are much cheaper, but you must be right. Buying deep ITM Options may sound expensive and risky, but it gives you a better path to where smart investors want to end up anyway, in a wheel. And with deep ITM Options, you will expose yourself to unlimited profits if you are very right.

Premium is King

I've put you through this washing machine of Options information. Your head might be throbbing considering all of the variables that go into Options trading. Greeks, underlying, legs, expirations. The one thing I want you to come away from this book is knowing one thing. Premium is King. Premium is what drives the Options market. Premium is what dictates what will give you the most long-term success. Premium is the one metric that wags your risk vs benefit profile. Premium answers this one question.

"Is the premium worth the trade?"

Is the risk I'm putting on the table worth the long-term risk? Notice I said "long-term." I firmly believe that using Options as a long-term tool maximizes any long-term investment strategy.

This warrants repeating. When you think about wealth generation through investing, you think about accumulating assets. It can be homes, stocks, or jewelry. As these assets accumulate, they will start paying you through rent, dividends, and covered calls. Options strategies like the Wheel force you to buy Low and sell High. Isn't that the point of investing? Buying assets on the cheap and selling them at a higher price. Using this philosophy, Options traders should never be afraid of taking on the responsibility of the Options contract. In other words, don't be afraid of selling Options. Remember the example of car insurance? In your personal experience, who pockets the most money; the insurance company or the car owner? Of course, it's the insurance company. They wouldn't be in business if they didn't come out on top. You can be the insurance company. Ultimately, the collected premiums will drive your profits.

The same goes for selling Options.

Before executing any short Option trade, ask yourself, "Am I prepared to take on the responsibility if it went ITM?" If you're a long-term trader, that answer should be "Yes, I'm prepared to take on the responsibility."

Final Practice Questions!

What characteristics are NOT typical of a vertical spread?
1. One BTO leg & one STO leg
2. Same underlying
3. Different expirations
4. One Call and one Put

Vertical Spreads are limited risk trades.
1. True
2. False

Which two vertical spreads collect a credit?
1. Bull Call Spread
2. Bear Put Spread

3. Bear Call Spread

4. Bull Put Spread

Iron Condors and Iron Butterfies are made up of what?

1. Bear Call Spread + Bull Put Spread

2. Two Bear Call Spreads + One Bull Put Spread

3. Two Bull Put Spreads

4. One Bull Call Spread + One Bull Put Spread

Iron Condors have a narrower profit zone compared to an Iron Butterfy.

1. True

2. False

A common % of profit to close an Iron Condor is what?

1. 20%

2. 50%

3. 80%

4. 100%

The Wheel starts with a Cash Secured Put.

1. True

2. False

To keep track of a Wheel use what?

1. Market analysis

2. Macroeconomics

3. Cost Basis

4. Balance Sheet

Rolling Out means to?

1. Close current position and re-establishing with a shorter-term expiration.

2. Close current position and re-establishing with a longer-term expiration.

3. Close current position and re-establishing with a different underlying.

Rolling Up means to?

1. Close current position and re-establishing with a higher strike.

2. Close current position and re-establishing with a lower strike.

3. Close current position.

Compared to an Iron Condor, a Covered Strangle collects?

1. More premium

2. Less premium

3. Equal premium

What three things does the Wheel accomplish?

1. Extra income from premiums.

2. Forces you to buy stocks at a discount.

3. Helps you predict stock price movement.

4. Forces you to sell stocks for higher gains.

Answers

What characteristics are NOT typical of a vertical spread?

1. One BTO leg & one STO leg

2. Same underlying

*3. Different expirations

*4. One Call and one Put

Vertical Spreads are limited risk trades.

*1. True

2. False

Which two vertical spreads collect a credit?

1. Bull Call Spread

2. Bear Put Spread

*3. Bear Call Spread

*4. Bull Put Spread

Iron Condors and Iron Butterfies are made up of what?

*1. Bear Call Spread + Bull Put Spread

2. Two Bear Call Spreads + One Bull Put Spread

3. Two Bull Put Spreads

4. One Bull Call Spread + One Bull Put Spread

Iron Condors have a narrower profit zone compared to an Iron Butterfy.

1. True

*2. False

A common % of profit to close an Iron Condor is what?

1. 20%

*2. 50%

3. 80%

4. 100%

The Wheel starts with a Cash Secured Put.

*1. True

2. False

To keep track of a Wheel use what?

1. Market analysis

2. Macroeconomics

*3. Cost Basis

4. Balance Sheet

Rolling Out means to?

1. Close current position and re-establishing with a shorter-term expiration.

*2. Close current position and re-establishing with a longer-term expiration.

3. Close current position and re-establishing with a different underlying.

Rolling Up means to?

*1. Close current position and re-establishing with a higher strike.

2. Close current position and re-establishing with a lower strike.

3. Close current position.

Compared to an Iron Condor, a Covered Strangle collects?

*1. More premium

2. Less premium

3. Equal premium

What three things does the Wheel accomplish?

*1. Extra income from premiums.

*2. Forces you to buy stocks at a discount.

3. Helps you predict stock price movement.

*4. Forces you to sell stocks for higher gains.

Chapter Eight

Taking the Plunge

Opening an Options Trading Account

N ow that you've grasped the fundamentals of Options trading, it's time to put your knowledge into action by opening your trading account. Some of the most well-known brokers that specialize in Options trading are:

- Tastytrade

- Charles Schwab/TD Ameritrade

- InteractiveBrokers

- E*TRADE

- Webull

For beginners, I suggest Tastytrade because they offer the easiest application process and platform. They built their software from the ground up, specifically with Options traders in mind. The drawback for Tastytrade is they don't offer paper trading. As a beginner, that could be a non-starter. Fortunately, they do have a very responsive support team. They'll be able to walk you through formulating a trade before hitting submit. On the other end is InteractiveBrokers. They offer a highly customizable platform for experienced traders. Day traders tend to prefer InteractiveBrokers. Of course, you may select any broker you wish. It may help to use the same broker as a close friend to have a quick and easy reference if you get lost. You'll find that the most challenging part of trading Options is turning theory into execution. The trading platform's ease of use will greatly enhance your trading execution. Oh, and don't forget to check out their fee structure. The good news is that with so much competition, most brokers have similar fees. Many offer very low-cost or even free trades. Thanks Robinhood. Check out any online videos and reviews that demo the various platforms. Once you've made your decision on a broker, get ready to apply.

Before going through the application process, make sure you have the following on hand:

- Social Security Number/card (SSN) or proof of ID number if not US citizen

- Your employer's name, address, and phone number

- Bank account numbers for funding purposes, plus routing number for check deposits.

Applying for Options trading privileges requires a little more input compared to opening a regular stock/investment portfolio. The broker will ask about your investment objectives. This usually includes income, growth, capital preservation, or speculation. They'll also want to know your knowledge of investing, how long you've been trading stocks or Options, how many trades you make per year, and the size of your trades. When the application asks, enter **2 Years of Experience**, **11-25 Trades per Year**, and **Limited Knowledge**. The exact verbiage per broker will differ. Entering those minimums will qualify you for most Options trades. Also, as a beginner, apply for a **cash account** or IRA account. Opening a margin account and accidentally executing a trade you can't handle could ruin you financially. Start with a cash account and move up to a margin account when you've gotten several years of trading in your back pocket.

The entire application process should take about 20 minutes. In some cases, up to a week. It all depends on how easily the broker can verify your financial information.

Conclusion

N ow that you've seen Options fully broken down and what you can do with said Options, I hope you feel far less intimidated by them. If you think back to your very first schooling, I'm sure learning the 26 letters of the Alphabet took us all some time. But learning and fully understanding those 26 letters has to be achieved before we move on to learning to read. Why? Because those letters and the sounds they make, build every word in the English language.

Options are no different. Options are simple from a 30,000-foot view as there is a Call and a Put. But as you look from a 5-foot view as we did - you'll see that all those terms and rules build upon each Option trade. Just as the letters in each word serve a purpose, so does every leg of each Option.

Above all, remember this... Options are contracts. Plain and simple.

When you get lost, reference back to this book to do the quick math to evaluate each angle of that trade... calculate how much you can profit as well as how much you can lose. Reference back to this book to check the terms and what they mean. Check the expiration on every Option, and above all - always trade with money you can afford to lose. No trade is guaranteed.

Vertical Spreads, Iron Condors, Sell Puts, Buy Calls...all of these trade strategies are basically combinations of the four Options trades; Buy Call,

Sell Call, Buy Put, Sell Put. I liken Options to a DNA helix. DNA is made up of only four parts. Adenine, Thymine, Guanine, and Cytosine. If you combine these into a long chain, the genetic possibilities are endless. Options are the same way. Combine the four basic Options trades into varying underlyings, expirations, quantities, and strikes. Options DNA is infinite. With these infinite possibilities, you can hone your creativity into a powerful money-making machine.

Options are not complex, they are involved. But you now have the knowledge to start trading Options and heck - you could even make a huge profit over time.

Good luck, and happy trading!

References

1. Admin, F. (n.d.). Which is the best time frame for Options Trading? https://app.fintrakk.com/article/which-is-the-best-time-fr ame-for-options-trading

2. Annuity.org. (2023, March 22). Saving vs. Investing | The Pros and Cons of Each & Tools to Use. https://www.annuity.org/personal-finance/investing/saving-vs-i nvesting/#:~:text=Saving%20and%20investing%20are%20impor tant,a%20strategy%20for%20building%20wealth

3. Cain, S. L. (2022, April 11). Stock Market Guide: What Is It And How Does It Work? Rocket HQ. https://www.quickenloans.co m/blog/stock-market-101-stock-market-work

4. Chen, J. (2022, April 23). Option Margin: Definition, Requirements, How To Calculate. Investopedia. https://www.investopedia.com/terms/o/option-margin.asp#:~:t ext=Options%20margins%20are%20the%20cash,and%20vary%2 0based%20on%20option

5. De La Fuente, P. (2023, March 31). How To Trade Options. NerdWallet. https://www.nerdwallet.com/article/investing/ho w-to-trade-options

6. Downey, L. (2023a, March 15). 10 Options Strategies to Know. Investopedia. https://www.investopedia.com/trading/options-s trategies/

7. Downey, L. (2023b, March 31). Essential Options Trading Guide. Investopedia. https://www.investopedia.com/options-basics-tu torial-4583012

8. E., & E. (2022, September 21). Top 12 Options Strategies Every Trader Should Know. Elearnmarkets - Learn Stock Market, Trading, Investing for Free. https://www.elearnmarkets.com/blog/1 2-must-know-option-trading-strategies/

9. ETF vs Index Options. (n.d.). https://www.cboe.com/tradable_ products/cboe_minis/etf_options/

10. Exercising Options and Expiration - Macroption. (n.d.). https:/ /www.macroption.com/exercising-options-expiration

11. Financial Planning - Importance of Savings and Investment | HDFC Life. (n.d.). HDFC Life. https://www.hdfclife.com/insurance-knowledge-centre/investm ent-for-future-planning/importance-of-savings-and-investments

12. Gravier, E. (2022, April 8). What are ETFs and should you invest in them? CNBC. https://www.cnbc.com/select/what-are-etfs-s hould-you-invest

13. How to pick the right options expiration date | Fidelity. (2018, July 5). https://www.fidelity.com/viewpoints/active-investor/o ptions-expiration-date

14. In the Money vs. At the Money Options: An Example - Macrop-

tion. (n.d.). https://www.macroption.com/in-the-money-vs-at
-the-money-options-example

15. In the Money, At the Money, Out of the Money Options -
Macroption. (n.d.). https://www.macroption.com/in-at-out-of
-the-money-options

16. Jackson, A. (2022, July 29). Options vs. Stocks: Which Is Right
for   You?   NerdWallet.
https://www.nerdwallet.com/article/investing/options-vs-stocks
#:~:text=What%27s%20the%20difference%20between%20stocks
,a%20stock%20price%20is%20headed

17. James Royal. (2023, February 22). Options vs. stocks: Which one
is better for you? Bankrate. https://www.bankrate.com/investin
g/options-vs-stocks

18. James Royal. (2023a, February 22). 5 options trading strategies for
beginners. Bankrate. https://www.bankrate.com/investing/opti
ons-trading-strategies-how-to-beginners/

19. Jeffries, S. (2023, February 28). Options vs. Stocks: Which Is Best
for You? GOBankingRates. https://www.gobankingrates.com/i
nvesting/strategy/options-vs-stocks

20. Kaeppel, J. (2022, June 7). ETF Options vs. Index Options:
What's   the   Difference?   Investopedia.
https://www.investopedia.com/articles/optioninvestor/10/etf-o
ptions-v-index-options.asp#:~:text=An%20exchange%2Dtraded
%20fund%20

21. Kramer, L. (2022, May 20). An Overview of Bull and Bear Markets. Investopedia. https://www.investopedia.com/insights/dig

ging-deeper-bull-and-bear-markets/

22. Let's Talk Money! with Joseph Hogue, CFA. (2021, January 1). 5 Options Trading Strategies for Beginners [Higher Return, Lower Risk] [Video]. YouTube. https://www.youtube.com/watch?v= owZNEuYL_N0

23. Marquit, M. (2022, January 17). Are Long-Term or Short-Term Investments Better? The Balance. https://www.thebalancemone y.com/are-long-term-or-short-term-investments-better-2385918

24. McKenna, K. (2021, April 26). Trading Vs. Investing: Which Is Better For Long-Term Goals? Forbes. https://www.forbes.com/sites/kristinmckenna/2021/04/26/tra ding-vs-investing-which-is-better-for-long-term-goals/?sh=6c2a5 c7a48f9

25. Mitchell, C. (2022, March 3). Day Trading vs. Investing: What's the Difference? The Balance. https://www.thebalancemoney.co m/day-trading-versus-long-term-investing-4139868

26. Nuvama | Online Share Trading India | BSE Sensex Today Live | Indian Stock Market | Equity, Currency Derivatives. (n.d.). N u v a m a . https://www.nuvamawealth.com/investology/introduction-to-i nvesting-c6eaf4/difference-between-long-term-investing-and-tra ding-b72956

27. O'Shea, A., & Voigt, K. (2023, March 31). Stock Market Basics: What Beginner Investors Should Know. NerdWallet. https://www.nerdwallet.com/article/investing/stock-marke t-basics-everything-beginner-investors-know

28. Option Greeks - Macroption. (n.d.). https://www.macroption.com/option-greeks/

29. Option Intrinsic Value Explained - Macroption. (n.d.). https://www.macroption.com/intrinsic-value

30. Option Intrinsic Value Formulas - Macroption. (n.d.). https://www.macroption.com/option-intrinsic-value-formulas/

31. Option Moneyness - Macroption. (n.d.). https://www.macroption.com/option-moneyness

32. Option Time Value - Macroption. (n.d.). https://www.macroption.com/option-time-value/

33. Price, M. (2023, March 14). Bull vs. Bear Market: What's the Difference? The Motley Fool. https://www.fool.com/investing/how-to-invest/bull-vs-bear-market/#:~:text=A%20bull%20market%20is%20occurring,when%20the%20economy%20is%20shrinking

34. Scott, G. (2022, January 1). Iron Butterfly Explained, How It Works, Trading Example. Investopedia. https://www.investopedia.com/terms/i/ironbutterfly.asp

35. Smith, T. (2022, September 24). Types of Stocks. Investopedia. https://www.investopedia.com/types-of-stocks-5215684

36. Stock Option History - The Options Playbook. (n.d.). https://www.optionsplaybook.com/options-introduction/stock-option-history/

37. Strike Price and Intrinsic Value of Call Options - Macroption. (n.d.). https://www.macroption.com/strike-price-intrinsic-valu

e-call-options

38. Strike Price and Intrinsic Value of Put Options - Macroption. (n.d.). https://www.macroption.com/strike-price-intrinsic-value-put-options/

39. Strike vs. Market Price vs. Underlying Price - Macroption. (n.d.). https://www.macroption.com/option-strike-market-underlying-price/

40. The Tokenist. (2023, January 16). Call Option Explained (2023): Step-By-Step Guide. Tokenist. https://tokenist.com/investing/call-option/

41. What Is an Option? - Macroption. (n.d.). https://www.macroption.com/what-is-an-option/

42. Wolfinger, M. (2022, February 7). The Iron Condor. Investopedia. https://www.investopedia.com/articles/trading/08/flock-to-iron-condors.asp

Just a Reminder! Be sure to get your free gifts!

- Free Cost Basis Calculator!

- Free Options Pricing Helper!

Just scan or click the QR code below or!

http://freegift.simplifiedfor.com

Drop us a message on our Facebook page. Happy Investing!

Made in the USA
Las Vegas, NV
21 February 2024

86101205R00085